# The Light in the Prison Window

## The Life Story of Hans Nielsen Hauge

*By*
WILHELM PETTERSEN

SECOND AND ENLARGED
EDITION

*"A greater man than Hans Nielsen Hauge Norway never had."*
*—Alexander Kielland*

THE CHRISTIAN LITERATURE CO.
Minneapolis, Minnesota
1926

HANS NIELSEN HAUGE

# INTRODUCTION

## HANS NIELSON HAUGE
### NORWAY'S GREATEST MAN

In that new dawn which came to Norway in the
very first years of the nineteenth century and opened
the door to a new day, stands the figure of that remarkable peasant-boy and unique lay-preacher, whose
life and work this book is to describe. During a quarter of a century Hans Nielsen Hauge fills the historical canvas of Norway.

In his complete consecration, his tremendous earn-
estness, the clearness with which he conceived of his
task, the heroic devotion with which he gave himself
to its achievement, in his humility and self-denial, in
the fineness of his moral fibre, in his victorious faith
and lofty spirituality, this man stands head and shoulders above his fellow-countrymen.

Who is a nation's greatest man?

He who, in possession of the finest character and
the ability to render his people the noblest service
which it is possible for man to render, gives all he is
and has, to render such service.

What service did Hauge render Norway at the
beginning of the last century?

When rationalism and godlessness was almost uni-
versally prevalent, he called his people back to God.

At a time when men's thoughts were occupied
almost exclusively with the things of this world, and
not always the decent things, he awakened in men's

3

hearts a yearning for higher and better things. In an age when the official clergy, at least the vast majority of them, both denied outright the fundamental teachings of the Christian religion and lived in flagrant violation of their observance, he stood forth as a preacher and defender of the simple gospel of salvation. While his nation was steeped in sin and walked in darkness, he lived a holy, self-sacrificing life, walking humbly in his Master's steps.

While he suffered to the uttermost, was persecuted and maligned, cruelly and unjustly punished, imprisoned though entirely innocent of wrong-doing, he kept the faith, prayed for friends and enemies, asking only that God's will be done.

And, after having suffered imprisonment for seven years, when he found his country in distress, he offered his services where he knew they would benefit the very government that had shut him up behind the bars.

Is not this the greatest and holiest service any man can render his people and his country? Hauge's power as a preacher, amazing as it was, was all but equalled by his keen insight into his country's economic and industrial need. Accused of being an idler, a vagabond, a tramp, he was perhaps the first man in Norway to see the great latent possibilities in the forests and mountains, the rivers and waterfalls, the bogs and the sea of his native country.

Wherever he went, he tried to point to some work that might be done to develop the resources of Norway.

The paper-mills he built, the salt-works he established, the mercantile enterprises he founded, the colonizations he started in out of the way places demonstrate that Hans Nielsen Hauge is the founder of the modern industrial life of Norway. To have changed the religious complexion of a country, to have been the prime cause of reforms that embraced its religious, moral, ecclesiastical and civil life, to have started a movement that changed its system of government from class-government to a government of the people, by the people, and for the people, to have created a demand for popular education, does not this entitle a man to be placed among the heroes of the nations?

And Hans Nielsen Hauge was just such a man. Only a farmer-boy! Only a lay-preacher! Only a fanatic and a dreamer!

Yes, but this farmer-boy and lay-preacher and dreamer—for fanatic he was not—is today looked upon as Norway's greatest man.

# CHRISTIANITY INTRODUCED INTO NORWAY

## PAGANISM—CATHOLICISM—THE REFORMATION

Officially, Christianity was introduced into Norway by the hero-King, Olaf Tryggvason. But paganism dies hard. Far into the nineteenth century clear evidences are found of a lingering paganism.

On the Fladeland farm in Upper Vraadal there stood as late as 1785 an image called Torbjorn. It had neither arms nor legs, but a human head, with eyes made of tin. The top of the head was open so as to allow for a large bowl into which beer was poured every Christmas. Each Saturday night it was washed and placed in the chief seat at the table. Similar images were found in other places also. One of these was not destroyed till the year 1857. In every distant valley superstitions built on paganism were rife among the simple-minded country folk.

The Reformation was introduced into Norway—also officially—in 1537; but Catholicism, which had taken the place of paganism, remained in faith and practice till late in the nineteenth century in many of the inland districts. Here and there were found shrines that were looked upon as very effective in curing diseases. The one best known in late times was a life-size crucifix found in the old "stave-church" at Roeldal.

It was worshipped especially at midsummer, on the fourth of July, according to the old chronology.

A Lutheran dean of the district in 1835 witnessed

7

a worship of this crucifix at a midnight service. He was just retiring for the night when, to his astonishment, he heard the church bells ringing. From his window he saw the church all lit up. Quickly dressing, he hurried to the parsonage, roused the minister, and together they walked to the church, where they found a crowd of people up near the altar, on which stood six wax-candles, while incense was being burned, filling the chancel with "holy smoke." The two ministers remained quietly in the church, watching the performance.

After the singing of a hymn, a discharged school-teacher read from a book of sermons belonging to the church a severe arraignment of—peculiarly enough—all papal worship. This ended, two men took down the crucifix, placed it against the altar, and each one present approached the crucifix and with a linen cloth wiped the "sweat" from its brow and face. The linen cloth was kept as a relique and was supposed to possess magical power to cure diseases. The pilgrims—for such they were all of them, except the old teacher and the two men who owned the church—were to take the linen cloths home with them. After this, the crucifix was again placed over the chancel, an offertory was intonated, and all the "pilgrims" laid a silver-offering on the altar. One man, who had come all the way from Holemdal, in the Bergen diocese, offered as much as ten dollars. All but one dollar, which the teacher was to get for his service, went to the owners of the church. Then a hymn was sung, after which the pilgrims hurried away, as they must needs enter the Roeldal district after sundown and leave it again before sunrise. In the Nesland church, Vinje, Tele-marken, the people of the district worshipped an image of the Virgin Mary, believing that their diseases would be cured. At this church, as well as at a couple of other churches, heaps of crutches were found, left there by pilgrims who had gone away cured.

In many places were "sacred springs," where the sick bathed, throwing their silver coins into the water, and this treasure was left untouched, like that of "Haug's" spring in Eidsberg, till the Swedes appropriated the money in 1814.

But paganism and catholicism were not the only difficulties with which an attempt to introduce a "living Christianity" into Norway had to contend.

The tremendous upheaval which was caused by the Reformation in other countries of Europe was hardly noticed in Norway.

The causes are not far to seek.

Norway lost its independence, when the last male descendant of the dynasty of Harold Fairhair (Haarfagre) died in 1319, and the country which for several centuries had played the chief role in the Scandinavian North, sank to be more and more a mere "appendage" of the Crown of Denmark.

The language in which were written the great Edda-songs and the Royal Sagas was split into dialects.

The leading aristocratic families died out, or were absorbed into the common peasantry—what centuries later was of great importance when the national spirit revived. Norway, which had been the most aristocratic of the Scandinavian countries, became the most democratic. The kings arrogated to themselves all authority, and Danish noblemen and office-holders got possession of the large estates.

Laws were promulgated in the Danish language, and when the Reformation was introduced into Norway by royal decree in 1537, it meant that there would follow the Bible in Danish, and Danish ministers, or Norwegian ministers educated and ordained in Denmark, would preach Danish sermons.

9

It is one of the most humiliating abdications of sovereign rights and national independence recorded in history. All the more so because it took place without a hand being lifted or a voice raised in protest.

Under these circumstances, the people of Norway would feel no more interest in the change of religion from Catholic to Protestant than if the king had ordered them to wear suits of blue instead of gray. The Catholic priests changed into Lutheran ministers over night.

In this miserable national abdication there is hardly a gleam of light, and no phase of it seemed more complete than that which pertained to religion and the church.

While in other countries literature and arts flourished, while the chariots of war rumbled through Europe from one end to the other, and new sciences were born that would some day make complete revolutions in men's minds, Norway slept peacefully under its ice-blanket of indifference.

As the state-church of Denmark—for Norway had no church of its own till 1814—increased in power and arrogance, the chief concern of bishops and ministers was to preach obedience to the reigning monarch of Copenhagen, who was the chief church dignitary, whether a pietistic and well-meaning man like Christian the Sixth (1730-1746), or a near-libertine like Frederick the Fifth (1746-1766), or a half-insane nondescript like Christian the Seventh.

The bishops swore allegiance to the king first of all. The gospel was of secondary importance.

The king appointed the bishops. The ministers were sometimes privately called to some beneficed parish, or called by the mayors and his council in the cities and towns, but in the country he was called by the dean in conjunction with some electors chosen by the people, i. e., some leading men in the parish.

To be a minister was to hold a job from the government, not to serve a congregation.

Even at best, the Reformation made slow progress. The common people continued for a long time to cling to the old worship, at times openly in defiance of law and government, at times clandestinely. As we have already noticed, images were worshipped, candles and incense burned, pilgrimages to sacred shrines made, and even pagan gods venerated up till the middle of the nineteenth century.

These, of course, were exceptions that became rarer and rarer, but it goes to show how old was the leaven that had to be thrown out. In many places the new Protestant worship caused violent opposition. Here and there the ministers sent out by the government were driven away from their churches, at times murdered by the enraged people.

Nor was either their morality or their ability such that they could expect to win the confidence and affection of the common man.

It was even possible for a minister who had openly committed murder to continue as officiating pastor. Drunkenness and other vices were common during the whole of the Reformation century, and even much later.

The seventeenth century is supposed to show some progress along reformatory lines, chiefly in taking away from the parishes all influence upon the choice of a pastor, and placing—in this respect as well as in all other respects—absolute power in the hands of the king, or of whomsoever he would graciously commission to act in his place.

The reason why this was regarded as an improvement was that the most unworthy considerations had come to play a prominent part in the choice of pastors. Sometimes a candidate in order to be favorably considered might have to agree to a material reduction in his stipulated income. Another candidate might offer the congregation a bribe to be accepted as a pastor.

A third was chosen because he chanted the collects to the tune of a "heroic ballad."

In parish after parish the son succeeded the father in the office, as if it were a farm or a business. If not, then the unmarried candidate must marry the widow of the deceased minister.

The question of ministers' widows, then as now, was a difficult one to solve. The above mentioned procedure made it easy to avoid the question. In many cases it was but natural for the candidate to marry the minister's daughter.

A very interesting story is told in this connection.

The daughter of the parish-priest of Bjornor was affianced to a student or curate. According to the prevailing custom, this young man should have received the "living" of the deceased minister. For some reason or other, some one else was chosen, and he received not only the "living," but the daughter to boot. However, when the minister in question died sometime after, the former was installed as his successor, and married his former fiancee.

These conditions were largely changed when, in 1660, the King of Denmark, by the help of the clergy and the burghers, became—as has been said—the most absolute ruler of Europe next to the Sultan of Turkey.

Among other things, he alone had the right to appoint clergymen to "livings," which almost as a matter of course, he continued to do with fond regard for the established custom of permitting son to succeed father, in some cases for a whole century. Or the son-in-law succeeded to the "living," or the deceased pastor's widow married her husband's first, at times also his second, and even his third, successor. An admirable system, indeed, where the sole aim should be to get an able, conscientious, and spiritual-minded preacher and pastor.

This second century (the seventeenth) after the Reformation is known as the century of Orthodoxy.

Learned and unlearned, peasant and nobleman, king and subject, all were equally "strong in the faith," as far as doctrine was concerned, and any form of heresy was the worst of crimes.

Murder could be atoned for with a fine, if it were taken any notice of at all. But woe to him who dared to question the smallest particle of the accepted doctrine imposed by the king. He was excommunicated and banished from the country. People would listen patiently to a sermon lasting for five hours. But as this sermon might be one of which the common man understood little or nothing, no wonder he took his revenge by indulging afterwards in a revelry that lasted twice as long.

Orthodoxy with a certain kind of ceremonial godliness went hand in hand and hand in glove with the grossest forms of dissipation, and it would be a mistake to think that the people left their ministers far behind in these matters.

Murderous duels, endless legal battles for the possession of property, and a more than half pagan mode of life were common things.

The minister might, in the interest of orthodoxy, as later in the interest of rationalism, thunder from his pulpit scathing denunciations against vice and crime, and the people took it good-naturedly as something it was the minister's business to do. They might even commend his severity and say: "Today Father was quite sharp," meaning thereby that it was a good thing to get such a "rubbing down" once in a while.

13

The worst samples of sermons left us from this wonderful period of orthodoxy are the obituary sermons. Some of them must have lasted five hours. First came a general introduction about death and related things. Then followed a long sketch of deceased's life from the cradle to the grave. Finally, a lengthy sermon on the text chosen for the occasion, filled to overflowing with Biblical quotations from Genesis to Revelation, illustrations, theological dissertations, even quotations in Latin and Greek from the church fathers.

Into such an obituary sermon the learned minister could pour anything in heaven, on earth, and under the earth, all he knew of history, fable, science, and mythology.

He might discourse on "sympathetic and antipathetic winds, the Egyptians, the Indians, the Sibylline books, Alexander the Great, Julius Caesar, and Emperor Augustus, Charles the Great, the geometrical lines of Archimedes, and anything else that might happen to strike his fancy."

The whole seventeenth century is filled with stories of ministers with whom drunkenness was habitual, of personal fights between the parish priest and his curate, with drawn knives and loaded guns, of clergymen who enter into public brawls with their parishioners with bare knives.

It is quite true that the clergy here and there worked hard to rectify these evils; but the evil was inherent in the state-church system, which left a deep chasm between the minister and his flock.

They had nothing in common, they never mingled socially. The minister was a superior person, the parishioner a subject. And, to make matters still worse, the minister was a foreigner, who spoke a language that the parishioners hardly understood. Could a church work under much worse conditions than those which prevailed in Norway from 1537 to near the end of the seventeenth century?

All the more grateful ought we to be that there were a few shining examples of true evangelical piety, like the Danish chancellor, Jens Bjelke, who though a high nobleman and a layman, wrote an exposition of the Lord's Prayer, which, so Dr. A. Chr. Bang says, shows "an unusual richness of thought as well a deep religiousness."

And, speaking generally, in spite of these discouraging conditions, it is during this very century that the seed was sown which was to produce that deep reverence for the Word of God that ever since has characterized the Norwegian people.

It is even historically correct to say that the last quarter of the seventeenth century saw the marshaling of the forces which a century later were to grapple in a fight to the bitter end.

This age is that of Louis the Fourteenth of France, when loose manners, disrespect for morality and religion, and denial of the fundamental tenets of Christianity swept through every country of Europe, as a fire sweeps the prairies of the West or goes roaring through the forests of Minnesota or Oregon and Washington. It left the upper social crust seared and all but denuded of moral principles and religious convictions of any kind, save for a remnant of deistic faith, as cold and withering as the wind that blows down from the frozen North.

It finally runs into that stark rationalism and rank materialism which characterize the eighteenth century.

Fortunately, it was not left unchallenged.

In the midst of this period of dead orthodoxy, voices cried out in the wilderness, like those of Johan Arnd

15

and Christian Scriver, followed by men like Spener and Francke. These great German theologians demanded that Christianity show its fruits in holy living, that faith must bear evidence of its genuineness by producing good works, that a faith which is not charitably active is a dead faith, that it is all very well to speak of the right kind of faith, but that it is equally important to speak of the right kind of life.

During the eighteenth century, Pietism, started by Spener and his friends, gained a strong foothold in Germany, Denmark, Sweden, and ultimately in Norway.

In spite of its one-sidedness, its separatistic tendencies and ultimate externalism, it brought to the Lutheran Church an awakening that was sorely needed, and carried on its shoulders the dawn of a new day which all of God's children hailed with rapturous joy.

Deplorable as the pietistic movement must be considered at its first appearance in the capital of Norway, with its contempt for the church and her ministers, for baptism and the Lord's Supper, and its declaration that the church was an institution of anti-Christ, it is entirely unfair to judge it even in its most unchurchly extravaganzes, except in the light of the worse conditions within the church itself.

Can anything more deplorable be conceived than a church whose ministers revel in drunkenness and worldliness, and whose lay members are admitted to the Lord's Table indiscriminately, regardless of what kind of life they lead, and who are finally sent to heaven in a five-hour sermon about "sympathetic and antipathetic winds," accompanied by Julius Caesar and the Emperor Augustus?

But pietism in Norway does not need a negative apology. Its real representatives are among the best ministers Norway ever had, and its fruits are the finest that ever grew on the tree of the gospel of Christ the Redeemer.

Through it, souls were saved, life was sanctified, missions were started.

The famous "Pleiades" (Syvstjernen) of the Church of Norway, consisting of Thomas von Westen, Amund Bartow, Eiler Hagerup, Jens Juel, Nikolai Engelhart, Peder Stroem, and Ments Ascanius are brilliant stars in the firmament of God's Kingdom.

In earlier times it was Bergen and Stavanger, where the gospel had found—and ever since then has found —its most zealous preachers. This time it was beautiful Romsdalen, that became the scene of an activity that is unique in the history of the church of Norway, until that man arose whom God called to make a conquest of Norway for Christ, alongside of which the conquest of Harold Fairhair pales into comparative insignificance.

Under the leadership of Thomas von Westen, these men set to work "to build the walls of Zion." Together they sent to the king a petition "that a commission of three be appointed to consider their proposal of a way to raise again the fallen-down Christianity."

Among other things, they propose a revival of church discipline, the establishment of a separate ecclesiastical court for the adjudication of all church matters, a reformation of the study of theology at the University of Copenhagen, that all who are appointed ministers must be persons capable of administering this office "as becomes a right-minded clergyman," that confirmation be introduced, and that more diligence and care be bestowed on the catechumenical instruction of the children.

Even if it be true that this "demonstration"—or gesture as we should call it today—brought very little

17

in the way of practical results, even if we admit that the proposals are too much concerned with external reforms, and legal enactments, the seed was sown which later bore manifold fruit.

And it is the first distinct voice from the church of Norway since the Reformation was introduced. Confirmation was introduced in 1746.

Dr. Erich Pontoppidan, known as the pietist bishop of Bergen, wrote his epoch-making Explanation of Luther's Catechism, by means of which, since its issue in 1737, thousands upon thousands of catechumens in Norway and America have received the most beneficial and life-determining instruction in the Christian religion.

The Bible was given wider circulation.

Thomas von Westen became the Apostle of the Lapps in the Far North, as Hans Egede later became the Apostle of Greenland. Needless to say that the high church dignitaries, especially the then bishop of Trondhjem, Dr. Peder Krog, did not understand and could not appreciate this new movement, in spite of the fact that the government of Denmark—which was also governing Norway—was thoroughly pietistic during the reign of King Christian the Sixth.

It was during this reign that the ecclesiastical rescript of January 13, 1741, known as the Conventicle Act, was issued.

The rescript was a well-meaning attempt to counteract the unchurchly influence of the religious movement which in church history is called Herrnhutism (Moravian Brethren). The king and his councillors were no doubt actuated by a genuine Christian zeal to propagate Christian knowledge and life among the common people. Briefly stated, the chief purpose of the rescript was twofold: "To protect those who evinced true solicitude for the edification of themselves and others from persecution, and secondly, to prevent the disorder arising from those who under the cloak of greater religiousness left their natural calling and wandered about from place to place as preachers without having either a divine or human call to do so. Ministers would be permitted and were encouraged to hold meetings (conventicles) in private houses, if only they saw to it that these meetings did not react injuriously upon the regular worship in the churches.

At these meetings, others might air their opinions, ask questions, and seek information, provided it did not bring about debates, but was carried on with decorum and in meekness.

At these meetings, the minister himself, or in his place some competent student of divinity, should invariably be present. Others might also hold similar conventicles, but attendance was restricted to very few, and these must always be of the same sex. Men and women together were not permitted to hold such meetings. Time and place should be reported to the minister of the parish who was to exercise due supervision over them.

Family devotion was to be encouraged; but strangers must not be present at these, at least only to the number of from one to three, and then only in exceptional cases. Any disturbance of such meetings was to be severely punished.

Ministers were earnestly exhorted to do their duty as pastors, and those who neglected the care of souls were to be warned and punished. In this way, these private meetings were to be made part and parcel of the pietistic state—church, but were to be carefully supervised and held within bounds by the official clergy. All other conventicles were prohibited, whether attended by many in public, or held secretly, or in the open air, or without having been duly sanctioned.

Men and women, who were unqualified as teachers or preachers of the Word of God, were not to be permitted to expound the Word in such gatherings. No man or woman must travel about as an evangelistic worker from place to place, but each one must remain in his legitimate calling, live quietly, make his or her living honestly, and eat his own bread.

Such were, in the main, the provisions of this famous Conventicle Act, and it was this Act which was used against Hans Nielsen Hauge and was responsible for his martyrdom.

It may or may not be pertinent to ask the question, "What would the Danish Government and the church officials of Norway have done to Hauge, if this Conventicle Act had not been such a convenient instrument ready at hand to be used in an endeavor to crush this man of God in his fearless and calm determination to awaken, with the help of God, a new life in the then moribund state church of Norway?"

The question can hardly be answered. We do not know. Persecutions against those who in any way "disturbed the peace" of the church were common enough in all lands.

Such persecutions fill the pages of church history all through the Middle Ages. The Edict of Worms, issued against Martin Luther, was a convenient instrument in the hands of the Catholic hierarchy for crushing Protestantism. Every tendency to follow in the steps of Luther was considered a crime to be punished with imprisonment, expatriation, and confiscation of property. Such fate befell many in Bavaria, Brandenburg, Saxony, Austria, the duchy of Mayence, and Salzburg, as well as in Hungary, Bohemia, and Poland. The Inquisition is no doubt the cruelest, the most barbarous and tyrannical institution ever invented for this purpose. Death sentence was often the penalty visited upon those who dared to hold religious views divergent from the official church dogmas. It was precisely similar persecutions that caused the massacre of St. Bartholomew Night in Paris and drove the French Huguenots—between three and four hundred thousand of them—out of France, to find asylums in Holland, Switzerland, England, Ireland, Prussia, and America, in all of which countries these brave Protestants became a beneficial ferment of the countries in which they settled. France, at the same time, lost some of its ablest, wealthiest, most industrious, and devotedly religious people, while much of the free-thinking that preceded and to a great extent caused the French Revolution was the result of apostacy among those Huguenots, who, to remain in France, violated their consciences and outwardly conformed to a religion that their souls abominated. Their descendants became skeptics and infidels. The story of the Salzburgers is especially noteworthy and enlightening.

Just forty years before Hauge was born, a company of Salzburgers, driven from their homes in beautiful Salzburg, an Alpine country of South Germany in many of its natural features resembling Norway, moved northward to settle in Prussia at the invitation of Frederick William the First.

"In the midst of winter with such horses and wagons and such provisions as they could command, they set out on their long journey. Their journey, though full of hardships, through Protestant countries, was almost a continuous ovation. Many companies were invited to settle at places on the way, but they had been invited to Prussia, and to Prussia they went. Nearly twenty thousand reached Prussia and a large

21

majority settled in Lithuania. The royal treasury was heavily taxed to provide for them while they were becoming self-supporting, but the king was well repaid by their contribution to the evangelical zeal and the economic forces of the country.

The King of England asked evangelical people everywhere to contribute to the relief of the emigrants, and the sum of nine hundred thousand florins was collected. A small colony of these Salzburgers settled in Georgia, where they have been noted for their thrift and their evangelical character.

It was from these Salzburgers that John Wesley, during his work in America, learned about the true evangelical faith, and it was from contact with the Moravian Spangenberg that he became acquainted with the Lutheran doctrine. On his return voyage, the Moravian minister, Peter Böhler, was his fellow passenger, and John Wesley was led by him to trust in Christ as his Savior and to experience the assurance of his sins forgiven. His conversion occurred in London at a meeting of the Moravian Brethren, where the introduction to Luther's commentary on Romans was being read. Thus Wesleyanism, or Methodism as it is now called, was born of Lutheranism. Verily, "God moves in a mysterious way His wonders to perform."

All this will help us to understand the way in which God led Hauge to become the great evangelist of Norway, and also to see how the stupidity of a Christian— even a Lutheran—government and church ultimately worked the will of God quite against their original purposes.

If a parallel should be drawn between the so-called Haugenism, both as to its effects upon Norway and as to its religious influence upon the Norwegian Lutheran Church in the United States, and any other similar movement, the Salzburg movement would stand us in good stead. For suppose—as was actually contemplated—that the friends of Hauge had been treated as were the Huguenots and the Salzburgers, what a tremendous loss in every way the country— poor enough as it was—would have suffered!

Norway has had many splendid bishops, both before Hauge's time and after.

This is especially true of the pietistic era in Norway. Between 1730 (the year of the Salzburgers) and 1778, when Hauge was seven years old, Norway had a line of bishops that form a beautiful galaxy of truly devoted men.

Peder Hersleb was bishop of the diocese of Christiania in 1730-1737.

Jacob Kærup, Jens Spidberg and Ole Tidemand were bishops of the diocese of Christianssand between the years 1733 and 1778. Erich Pontoppidan was bishop of the Bergen diocese from 1748 to 1755, and Frederich Arentz from 1762 to 1774, followed by that staunch friend and defender of evangelical truth, even of Hauge, Johan Nordal Brun.

In the Trondhjem diocese, Eiler Hagerup was bishop from 1731 to 1743 and Ludvig Harboe from 1743 to 1748.

One wonders what Hauge's revival would have become, if in his day these men, or men like them, had been bishops in Norway, instead of such intolerant, rationalistic, and unevangelical bishops as Christen Schmidt and Fr. Julius Bech in Christiania, Dr. Peder Hansen in Christianssand, Johan Chr. Schoenheyder in Trondhjem, and Mathias Bonsach Krogh in Tromsoe. These latter were not only opposed to Hauge as a lay preacher, but, though bishops in a Lutheran church, they were outspokenly opposed to Christianity itself.

In the very nature of things, one should have expected a revival from the work of such men as Pontoppidan, Arentz, Irgens, and Brun, and from ministers as devoted to the cause of Christ as Dr. Theol. Hans Strom at Eker, the famous dean at Ullensvang in Hardanger, Niels Hertzberg, Johan Sebastian Cammermeyer in Bergen, and a few others in the eastern part of Norway.

In the very nature of things, a revival could be least expected just at the time it did come, when bishops ridiculed Christianity, and ministers, instead of preaching the gospel of salvation, talked about planting potatoes, about vaccination, wrote drinking-songs, and made their parsonages into factories of scientific instruments, said that faith was the same as "common sense," that the "Explanation" of Pontoppidan was a "bad" book, while a Danish baron, Wedel, proposed that the whole clergy should be gotten rid of.

Once more we shall see—and how constantly we need to be reminded of it—the truth of what has been so beautifully expressed in that well-known hymn of Cowper:

> "God moves in a mysterious way
> His wonders to perform:
> He plants His footsteps in the sea
> And rides upon the storm.
>
> Deep in unfathomable mines
> Of never-failing skill,
> He treasures up His bright designs,
> And works His sovereign will.
>
> His purposes will ripen fast,
> Unfolding every hour.
> The bud may have a bitter taste,
> But sweet will be the flower."

Surely, "Not by might, and not by strength, but by my spirit," saith the Lord.

All the orthodox and pietistic ordinances of the

Danish government during the reign of King Christian the Sixth could not avail to produce a single true, living Christian. They did produce a "sterile form" of outward Christianity that soon became a caricature of the very thing they aimed to produce. Churchism, ceremonies, fine music are beautiful adjuncts of Christianity. Forms may be the expression of life within, but just as often may be like the flowers that conceal death. They cannot produce life.

Again, the Lord has His own time, and—with reverence be it said, also with profound respect for all sincere efforts exerted in the interest of God's Kingdom—the Lord chooses His own instruments, at times with astounding disregard of what we should expect.

No doubt the Lord loves a true bishop, as He loves every true servant in His Church, but in choosing His man for a great task, He has a most disconcerting way of passing by that which is high in the world as well as what is prominent in the Church, and to take the one least thought of: a little shepherd-boy of the small tribe of Benjamin to be the greatest King of His Chosen People, a rabid, persecuting pharisee to be the greatest of Apostles, a Saxon monk to be the greatest church reformer, an English shoemaker to be one of the greatest of missionaries, two Norwegian peasant boys to be the leading missionaries in foreign lands of the Norwegian Church, a rail-splitter from Kentucky to be America's greatest president. A man may be well fitted for the administrative work of a bishop, keenly interested in all matters pertaining to the orderly and faithful performance of pastoral duties, actuated by the highest motives, diligent, upright, painstaking, self-sacrificing, learned, and eloquent, yet not the man to arouse a nation.

To find such a man, God may pass by kings and bishops and ministers and doctors of theology and professors and all the great, shining lights of learning and culture, with their fine robes and white hands and elegant manners. He may say, "The work that I am going to have done now is one for which none of you are fitted. You may wear crowns and mitres and white robes, you may deliver eloquent sermons and write splendid commentaries, and build great cathedrals, but this time I have to find a man who can convert souls.

"He must be willing to obey Me, regardless of what men may say. The man I need is one who dares to stand up and say, humbly but fearlessly: 'We should obey God more than men.'"

God may say, "The bishop cannot do it, for he is bound by his allegiance to the king. The minister cannot do it; for it might cost him his 'living.' I can get no help from the diocesan prefect or the district judge for they are all tied up in a 'system.'"

These, again, might not be the true reasons. It is "hit and miss" with us in such things. Maybe the darkness was not dark enough. Maybe the difficulties were not great enough, so that if it were done, men might say, "We did it."

Who knows? What we do know is that in God's own way the soil was made ready.

During 250 years after the Reformation, ignorant and ungodly ministers, learned and pious ministers, drunkenness and dissipation, piety and purity, dead orthodoxy and fanatical disregard of church and public worship and the sacraments, shifted and changed, till the day came when all was darkness, like that of Egypt as the Israelites left the country to follow Moses into the desert on the way to the Promised Land,—when rationalism, like dry-rot, had eaten itself into the hearts and minds of clergy and people.

And then God spoke through a peasant boy from Tune in Smaalenene.

26

# THE TIME OF HAUGE

## CONDITIONS IN NORWAY: ECONOMIC—MORAL—RELIGIOUS

But why should Hans Nielsen Hauge interest us now?

We are interested in Hauge because he is of our own flesh and blood, as typically Norwegian as Rosenius was typically Swedish, as Grundtvig was typically Danish, as Luther was typically German, as Wesley was typically English, as Paul was typically Hebrew.

Hauge is the one great outstanding religious type sprung right from the native soil of Norway. And wonderful as was the work done by the Monk from Wittenberg, we of Norwegian descent feel that we may to our profit seek our spiritual connections a little nearer home if we are to preserve the bit of independent spiritual life still left and fast vanishing, if we are not always to remain in spiritual vassalage, as we were in political vassalage during close to four centuries.

It has already been stated that Norway was very little touched by the Reformation. It was ordered introduced by a Danish king, preached mostly by Danish ministers and in the Danish language. In the wake of the Reformation there came, to begin with, a large number of very clever fortune-hunters and quite a number of poorly equipped ministers from Denmark.

The story is told of one minister that when a

parishioner came to see him, the minister would stand on the inside of a locked door, and, instead of "shaking hands" with him, had a small opening made in the door through which he thrust a piece of wood for the man to "shake."

This is both characteristic and symbolic of the general attitude of the foreign clergy to the common people long after the Reformation.

These foreign ministers did not understand the people any more than the people understood them. They were so hated by the people that in one parish in Telemarken seven of them were killed in quick succession, and one district, that of Aaseral, in southern Norway, was entirely without a minister for a long time. No Dane dared to live among them. This, of course, was not altogether to the credit of the people.

The first distinctly Norwegian assertion of a national spirit came with Hauge. The first genuinely Norwegian preachers were Hauge and his associates. Do we overlook him because he was "just a Norwegian farmer-boy," because he was not a German or a Dane?

Then we may as well be reminded of the fact that, largely due to the work of Hauge, quite a large number of really big men in Norway during the nineteenth century came from the same good soil of the peasantry as Hauge himself. Taking a random look at Norway's able men since 1814, as compared with the leading men of the previous century, we see that a great change has taken place. It is no longer Pontoppidan, Peder Hansen, Schoenheyder, Schmidt, Wilse, Bech, Bloch, Hount, Windfeld, Top, some of them very able men, but all Danes, and all but the first hardly fit men for an evangelical ministry. During the last years of the eighteenth and during the early nineteenth century we find such typical Norwegian men as Johan Nordahl Brun, Nicolai Wergeland, Jens Stub, Hersleb, Sverdrup, Keyser, Sorensen, Roennau, von der Lippe, Hagerup, Bugge, and then more and more coming direct from the common people, like Skrefsrud, Dahle, Bjornson, Lie, Garborg, Bergslien, Skeibrok, Skredsvig, Laache, Jorgen Moe, Landstad, Jaabæk, Ueland, Sivert Nielsen, Dr. Bishop A. Chr. Bang, Ivar Aasen, Vinje, Dr. Blix, and many others.

Or do we overlook him because, though Norway's greatest preacher, he had no academic education and was not an ordained minister?

Christians at least ought to be well enough acquainted with I Cor. 1, 26—2, 5 to know that God, in choosing His instruments, pays no attention to birth, or wealth, or rank, or human institutions.

Suppose we ask this question: "Which had the better right to preach the gospel in Norway, a man who, though a minister, did not believe in the fundamentals of the Christian religion, who went straight from the pulpit to the card-table, a theatrical performance, the ball-room, and the wine-cup, and who was appointed by a Danish king whose disorderly life made him insane, or one who, himself converted, burned in his soul to save others, who was strictly orthodox, and was willing to suffer death rather than disobey the Lord who had called him to be His messenger among his own people?

One more thing should be noted in order to understand Hauge and his work.

It is quite evident that Hauge saw the faults of the economic system of his day just as clearly as he saw the faults of the spiritual, moral, and social order, and he sought to correct the economic evil with all the means in his power.

The privileges of the mercantile class of the large

29

cities like Bergen, Stavanger, Christianssand, Arendal, Drammen, Trondhjem and Christiania weighed as heavily on the farmer and the fisherman as did the privileges of the government class. The merchant could offer them any terms he pleased, and they had to stand "hat in hand" and take what they got. The merchants did not scruple to skin the farmers of their districts of the last thing they had.

An old song from the time of Hauge's childhood (between 1770 and 1780) makes this quite clear.

One verse (freely translated) says:

"When they his goods have taken,
    These fleecers fierce and bold,
They carry home the bacon
    And big carousals hold.
Then drink they and make merry
    With theatre and ball,
But the blood-money of the farmer
    For sure must pay for all."

As Hauge became cognizant of this, he no doubt felt as did Abraham Lincoln when at New Orleans he witnessed the auctioneering of the negroes into slavery, and like him he may have vowed that if possible, he would make an end of it. And as it cost Lincoln his life to do away with slavery, so it practically cost Hauge his life to go against the monopolistic system of the Danish government and the privileged class of big business men of the larger cities of Norway. One may judge of conditions of that time by the fact that the inhabitants of Nordland, who had to buy their grain in Bergen, were in 1765 indebted to the magnates of that city in the sum of 300,000 dollars, which debt in 1807 had grown to the enormous sum of close to one million dollars.

In the southern county of Nedenes, the common man was in about the same condition of being the "bonded serf" of the mercantile houses of Christians-sand and Arendal, who cheated him outright, placed too low a price on the lumber the farmer sold to them, and instead of paying the farmer in money or in grain and other necessities of life, gave him bad brandy, bad tobacco, and the most useless articles at high prices. These things the farmer must sell at a low price in order to get money with which to pay his taxes and procure food and clothing.

When the debt grew too large, the merchant took the poor man's "book of credit," and with hard words and a kick drove him from the premises. Before he knew of it, he had to let his farm go and stood home-less with his family.

In Christiania there were certain lumber firms that deliberately refused to pay the farmer for the lumber he had delivered. When a humane diocesan sheriff, A. P. Levetzau in 1771 (the very year in which Hauge was born) was able to procure a royal decree forbid-ding these malpractices, he became "royally" hated by the city magnates for it.

In olden days, the king had prided himself that every citizen, preferably the free peasants of Norway, could approach him personally with their petitions for redress. This was forbidden during the reign of the pietist King Christian the Sixth, unless the com-plaint was "vised" by the county sheriff. If they came anyway, they were to be put in solitary confinement in the military prison. One may easily understand how this would work, since the sheriff might be the very man against whom the complaint was lodged.

The burden of taxation became at last unbearable.

Each farm was taxed for from ten to fourteen dif-ferent contributions to the king, and besides these there were contributions in grain or money to the district judge, the bailiff, the parish clerk, the parish beadle, the district attorney, the parish minister, school, and the poor.

The Norwegian farmer is proverbially patient, but even his patience will ultimately give out.

One straight-backed farmer at that time was Trond Lauperak in Bjerkreim, Dalene.

For a few years after he had come into possession of his ancestral farm, he paid his taxes like the rest. When, however, there came the demand for a large extra tax in 1762, Trond said, "No."

"The king," he said, "does nothing for Bjerkreim, then why should he have any tax from Bjerkreim? The money leaves the country and is only wasted. Frederick the Fifth is King of Denmark, but I am King of Bjerkreim."

There is the beginning of 1814 in this. It has in it the ring of the Boston tea-party. Of course, he paid the tax, anyway. But even he had, in his old age, to yield to the parish minister. The farmers of the parish did not like their new minister, a simon-pure rationalist, G. H. Reiner, because he swore too much and used contumacious language about the parents to the children of his catechumen class. He was, besides, suspected of heresy.

During a bishop's visitation in 1799, Trond Lauperak arose in the church, spoke on behalf of the congregation, and demanded the removal of the minister.

The farmers had agreed that they should all rise and support Trond. But while Trond spoke, the minister sat looking so fixedly at the congregation that not a man dared to rise. The bishop reprimanded the seventy-year-old spokesman—and praised the minister. Finally, after a year of crop-failure and failure of the fisheries, the people of Nordhordland gathered in Bergen, demanded to see the royal tax decree, seized the diocesan sheriff, Cicignan, removed his wig, tore his clothes, and dragged him into the street. This frightened the poor man so much that he repaid the taxes he had collected.

This is the famous "War of the Strils". The people in other districts did likewise, and many were imprisoned.

It is interesting to remember that this happened a few years before the American colonies rose in rebellion against the stamp tax imposed by an "overseas-king" and through the War of Independence won their freedom from English rule. Why did not Norway do the same? Evidently because the people of Norway lacked a real national leader.

If Christian Lofthus of Nedenes had been as wise and firm as he was brave and patriotic, Norway's independence might have dated from 1786 instead of from 1814.

Born at Risoer in 1750, Lofthus inherited a large farm in West Moland, near Lillesand, where also he owned a sawmill, a store, and was a ship-owner besides. In 1781 he received the first prize for improved farming from the Scientific Society of Trondhjem. His business enterprises brought him the hatred of the privileged city magnates, who were successful in ruining him financially.

In 1786 he twice visited Copenhagen in an attempt to lay before the Danish Crown Prince Frederick, who was regent during the insanity of Christian the Seventh, a petition for redress of grievances signed by 329 of the farmers in the diocese of Christianssand.

He was arrested in 1787, sent to the military prison of Akershus in irons, and a "Commission" sentenced him in 1792 to life imprisonment. Two years after his death, the Supreme Court confirmed this sentence. Lofthus died in prison in 1797, the year in which Hauge began his work of evangelizing Norway.

As we shall see later on, one of the chief accusations against Hauge was that he used his religious influence over the people for the purpose of enriching himself, an accusation as baseless in fact as it was malicious in motive.

Perhaps the authorities thought that Hauge was another Lofthus who under the mask of a religious campaign would cause a popular uprising.

It ought to help us "straighten our backs" to see this young man leave his plow and traverse Norway on foot from end to end till he had covered the whole country—see him sit down, at home or on his way or in prison, to pen simple, straightforward books of devotion, songs, letters, and sermons, without a dictionary or a commentary to help him, books which, just because they were simple and straightforward, went straight to the hearts of the simple-minded, comforting them in their sorrow, answering their questions, explaining their difficulties, making strong their faith, opening up to them the straight and narrow path to peace and life such as no other books at that time could do—see him lay the foundation of Norway's material progress in the establishment of factories and enterprises of diverse kinds, till he became a veritable "captain of industry" whom the privileged classes hated and the government feared.

Suppose the ministers of the Church of Norway and the government of the two countries had understood this man!

Suppose they had said: "You are just the man we have been looking for! You understand the people. Your eyes are open so that you can see opportunities for development and advancement. Go preach! Set men to work!"

What a mighty stir he might have made! What discoveries and inventions would have followed! Agriculture would have made Norway rich. Every city would have had a shipyard, every waterfall would have turned wheels of industry, looms would have kept people busy, roads would have been built—just fifty years before it actually happened.

But there is little use in "supposing" very much with such a government and such "blind men leading the blind."

And so they set to work to discourage, hamper, hinder, persecute, berate, deride, beat and imprison the only man who really knew his people and loved his country, till this big-hearted, warm-souled, clear-minded, strong-willed, sound-bodied man was a brokendown wreck, suffering from as many diseases as he had been years in prison.

Professor Sverdrup of Augsburg Seminary once said to the author: "It is very difficult not to feel contempt for humanity."

Thus have great souls and big minds suffered in all countries and in all ages.

The half-century in which Hauge lived is unique in history.

It covers almost exactly 50 years, from 1771 to 1824. Within this period more changes took place in the world at large, and in every civilized country, than at any other time of the same length. The events that occurred will tell the story better than any description of them can do.

Let us take our own country first, the United States of America.

The American War of Independence began with the Battle of Lexington in 1775. The next year came the Declaration of Independence. At the Peace of Versailles in 1783, England recognized this independence. The Constitution was ratified in 1788. In 1789 the new western Republic elected George Washington her first President. He was followed by John Adams in 1793, by Thomas Jefferson in 1801, by James Madison in 1809, by James Monroe in 1817, and by John Quincy Adams in 1825.

Two great inventions mark this eventful period, that of the cotton gin in 1793, and that of the first steamboat in 1807.

Among the world events of the very first magnitude, that of the establishment of the North American Republic ranks with the Exodus of Israel from Egypt, the rise and fall of the Roman Empire, and the Reformation, as one of the greatest, just as the Declaration of Independence is one of Humanity's Four Magna Chartas.

In the European world, the period is that of the French Revolution and the Napoleonic wars, which kept Europe in constant turmoil from 1789 till Napoleon was safely landed on St. Helena in 1815, after the battle of Waterloo. What with the downfall of the feudal aristocracy, the declaration of the Rights of Man, the consolidation of England, Scotland, and Ireland into one powerful state of Great Britain, the awakening of the spirit of nationalism, liberty, and independence, the rise of Prussia as the leading German state, the revolutionary ferment introduced into every country, the establishment of republics, and the tremendous impulse given to all the sciences, with cries for reforms rolling like angry waves of the ocean against thrones and class-privileges, Hauge's life-time is certainly one of the great historic periods.

In Denmark between 1771 and 1772, Struensee introduced some very important reforms. Freedom of the press was established, torture to compel confession of crime was abolished, and noblemen were no longer permitted to send their servants to Norway as high functionaries.

His successor, Ove Hoegh Guldberg, was indeed a reactionary who abrogated most of the reforms of Struensee, so that a police magistrate could fine any author or publisher without trial and at will. He wanted to hold the farmers down in serfdom; "for," said he, "if you give the farmer his liberty, it will shake the foundation of the state"; but he was at least a Dane, who spoke Danish, and introduced the mother-tongue into the army and the schools.

In 1776, it was decreed that only men born within the boundaries of Denmark could hold any public office.

It is from this age (1772-1784) we have the well-known Guldberg's hymn-book which was used extensively in Norway, while the common man clung to the hymn-book of Kingo, impregnated as these hymns were with a virile Christian spirit, while some wishy-washy stuff was taken into Guldberg's book, and still more into the impossible, unevangelical, and almost un-Christian "Evangelic Christian" hymn book, in which rationalism celebrated its triumph just before its fall.

Guldberg was succeeded as prime-minister in 1784 by the gifted Andreas Peter Bernstorff, during whose administration, from 1784 to 1797, "enlightenment" ruled high and low, and everything was to be done according to "reason."

The fundamental idea was that lack of education was the cause of immorality, vice, and crime, and that if people were only educated properly, they would become virtuous. But reason never made a worse "fiasco" than during the latter part of the eighteenth century. Poets were to be rewarded with prizes, and poetry sank to the most intolerable platitudes.

Ministers were to preach rationally and usefully, and in their sermons they told people to plant potatoes and similar useful things.

This "enlightenment" went so far that a certain Professor Gamborg of the University of Copenhagen proposed to introduce canary birds into the woods of Denmark, so that these foreign songsters might teach the Danish birds to sing. One good reform which Denmark owes to Bernstorff is the "Emancipation" of the Danish farmer from age-long serfdom. From now on the peasant was permitted to leave the place in which he was born without risking being flogged for it if captured, as had been the case hitherto. This was not needed in Norway where the farmer was as free in his person as the nobility in other countries. But the freedom of the press was still further curtailed, so that no one was permitted to print anything unless he put his name on the title page, and all smaller books should be sent to the police magistrate for examination before they were published.

In 1801 Denmark was awakened by the battle of the King's Deep and a great part of her fleet was destroyed by an English fleet under Parker and Horatio Nelson. The English returned in 1805, bombarded Copenhagen and sailed away to England with seventy Danish "men of war." Only forty-four ships, however, reached England. This was because Denmark refused to join England against Napoleon, but demanded the right to remain neutral. This high-handed act led to Denmark joining France, and finally brought about the separation of Norway and Denmark by the treaty of Kiel in 1814.

During the Napoleonic wars, Norway suffered from lack of grain. What little grain they had, they mixed with bark, and called it "bark-bread," and much sickness and even outright starvation was caused by these unjust trade-regulations. Henrik Ibsen's beautiful poem "Terje Vigen" describes one single episode from these terrible years, when English "men of war" tried their best to prevent Norway from obtaining grain from Denmark, in fact, tried to establish an actual blockade, with but little relief given by certain "licensed" ships. Altogether it was a trying time for Norway, just such a time as "tries men's souls," but perhaps also tend to arouse people to think about the welfare of their souls.

This certainly had a good deal to do with the success of Hauge, who for eight years, and up till his imprisonment in 1804, sowed the seed of the gospel, taught people frugality, sobriety, and industry, in short, self-help both spiritually and economically, and thereby broke the ground for Norway's independence in 1814.

For just at this time there appeared in Norway this mighty leader, who brought forth "water from the rock" to make a barren land live again.

Perhaps at no time in the history of Norway was such a man needed as just at this time.

The pervading spirit of Norwegian institutions and ideals, philosophy and religion was that of practical materialism, hard rationalism, and unreasonable self-complacency.

Deism, then religiously dominant, meant a vague belief in a God for the cultured few, with a very strict dogmatic system for the ignorant many.

The "state-church" must be preserved in order to secure the obedience of the common people.

But nothing can be worse for a Church or a religious system than a public adherence to its forms and a private ridiculing of its substance by a large portion of the governing class. The danger to the state-church was not that its precepts were not being avowed, but that they were ceasing to be believed among the upper class.

While the church became more and more a political machine, the state became less and less religious.

In the country parishes there were altogether too many clergymen who were utterly worldly, who looked too frequently and too deeply into the drinking bowl, did many other things, which they had not taken an oath to do, but did some things which they had taken an oath not to do. While speaking to the refined intellect of the few, they paid no attention to the unsavory multitude in homespun, who paid the tithes. A bishop could sit and listen to a minister preaching an attenuated gospel that had in it neither a Savior, nor remission of sin, nor repentance, nor sanctification, and just about no God, and say nothing, or even praise the minister's eloquence and learning. On the other hand, if he heard a minister speak about "the blood of Christ, which cleanseth from all sin," he would find this intolerably old-fashioned, something too coarse and brutal for the delicate ears of the "cultured class."

A governing class, and a clergy bent only on cards, balls, theatres, and wine, besides preferment and an increased income, were now to feel the force of a great religious wave which was to beat on every wall of privilege. These two classes were as utterly unable to understand a religious revival as if they had been so many blocks of wood. But when they felt their authority challenged and their privileges threatened, or, worse yet, their tithes reduced, then they did open their eyes and the blocks of wood became alive with wrath and hatred.

One of Norway's most famous bishops was Peter Olivarius Bugge, who was appointed to the diocese of Trondhjem in 1804, the year in which Hauge began his long and final imprisonment.

When once at a "visitation" the deacons complained

of a certain minister, especially of his sermons, he said: "The preachers that mix truth and error are dangerous. Your minister preaches only nonsense, and he is not dangerous."

What could one expect when even so evangelical a man as S. B. Hersleb, who was the first theological professor at the University of Christiania, undoubtedly an earnest and true Christian as he was a very learned theologian, understood the fourteenth article of the Augsburg Confession to forbid all lay preaching, an opinion which he inculcated into his theological students so thoroughly that most of them, after they became ministers, both privately and from the pulpit warned against a revival such as the one Hauge had started. This was sowing dragon's teeth in the religious soil of Norway, and it took another half century to clean the soil of these bitter roots which have caused so much misunderstanding, suspicion, and even enmity between the Norwegian clergy and laity.

A peculiar feature of this age of Hauge was that anything that savoured of originality or fervor was a matter of fear or suspicion, and was denounced as "enthusiasm." This use of the word "enthusiasm" as synonymous with fanaticism is characteristic of the age.

In an age when political stability was the chief aim of society, and when the clergy figured as a sort of spiritual "sanitary police," the use of the term is quite intelligible.

There was nothing of this in the Haugian movement. Looked at from the outside, it was the most peaceful movement imaginable.

Hauge walks along, singing and knitting a stocking or a pair of mits. He meets a man and speaks to him about this or that in every day life till he sees his chance to mention "God and salvation." The man in most cases becomes a seeker after God.

He arrives at a farm and takes a scythe or a rake and helps in the harvest. In the evening he assembles the people for worship. He says to a little lad, "You might become a child of God," and the lad remembers it as long as he lives.

As he enters a house, he uses the greeting, "Is all well in here?" And the two words "all well" create an atmosphere in which the Word of God works conversion.

His voice is like fine music, rich and warm. It reaches far and it searches deep.

He sees a waterfall, and he figures how much can be made out of it for the material benefit of the people of his country. He looks out over an audience, as they sit there in the evening twilight of the little cottage. He scans the faces of these hardy mountaineers, these descendents of kings and earls and chieftains from centuries back. He looks at these fine women with their softer features, beautiful as only Norway produces them, in their quaint costumes.

Or maybe the fire is just dying on the hearth and throws the light of its last fllickering flames up under the smoked rafters, till a log is placed on the fire so that it flares up again and reveals eager faces turned wonderingly towards this strange preacher in homespun. Then he, in turn, wonders how many of these are ready for the Kingdom. These scenes have been painted, by Tidemand, by Gausta, and others, exquisite scenes from the religious revival of Norway, which when seen are never forgotten.

# THE LIFE AND WORK OF HAUGE
## —CHILDHOOD AND YOUTH
### 1771-1797

The life of Hauge divides itself into four periods, each divided from the other by a distinct line of demarkation.

The first period lies between the years 1771 and 1797. This is the period of his childhood, youth, conversion, and call to be a preacher of the gospel.

The second period lies between the years 1797 and 1804. During this period Hauge did his great work of preaching, traveling, writing and publishing books, and laying the foundation for Norway's industrial life and economic progress.

The third period lies between the years 1804 and 1814. During these years Hauge was imprisoned in the capital of Norway, while waiting for his "case" to be tried, and a verdict rendered. These are the "years of want" in the history of Norway; perhaps the hardest years of suffering the Norwegian people ever experienced, as they are the years during which Hauge suffered more from cruelty, barbarism, and injustice than any other man in the whole range of Norwegian history.

The fourth period lies between the years 1814 and 1824, from the year of Hauge's release from prison to the year of his death.

These periods are uniquely seasonal. There are, first of all, the twenty-five beautiful years of springtime, of sprouting grass, budding trees, singing birds, and plowing of the soil.

Then comes the summer-life of eight years of constant evangelistic work, such as few men in the whole history of Christianity have done.

The third period of ten years is the fall, with storms, duress, and indescribable suffering — dark years during which Hauge's soul is enveloped in gloom, when his heart is near breaking, when his whole life seems to be a complete failure.

The fourth period of ten years is like the calm of a beautiful winter day in eastern Norway, years of vindication and final victory.

Hauge was born in the year 1771. His father was a comparatively well-to-do farmer at Rolf's Island in Tune parish, Smaalenene, not far from the city of Fredriksstad, in the extreme southeastern corner of Norway, and only a few miles from the Swedish boundary. Both father and mother were intelligent and deeply religious people. There was a large family of boys and girls, all of whom, with but one exception, were exceptionally gifted. Hauge lived with his parents till he was twenty-five years old. All through his early years, till the time of his confirmation. Hans, who was a quiet boy, was struggling with his inner self under the influence and guidance of the Holy Spirit. Yet he was of a practical turn of mind, and very early developed a strong inclination for business. At the same time he was also, as a Methodist would say, under a strong conviction of sin — very much like the great reformer, Martin Luther. Several times during his early youth he was at death's door from drowning in the river near by, and so became more and more serious, declining entirely to take part in the common amusements of the time. His companions regarded him as "peculiar." Everybody realized that he was unusually gifted. In his home was found the best Christian literature of the day, all of which the young boy read with eagerness. He himself mentions Luther's Catechism, the Explanation of Pontoppidan, Kingo's hymn-book, and the Bible; but his own writings make it a safe assumption that he was thoroughly familiar with Johan Arend's "True Christianity," Luther's and Muller's books of sermons, the "Mirror of Faith" by Pontoppidan, Collin's "Revelation of Christ in the Soul," and the "Rare Jewel of Faith" by Brorson.

How different he was from other boys of his day is best shown by what happened on his Confirmation Day. He was then past fifteen. His sister had difficulty in persuading him to dress properly, especially in getting permission to dress his hair according to the fashion of the day. When he met some boys on his way to the church, one of them said, "To-day Hans Nielsen has his hair dressed." "Yes," Hans answered, "if to-day we have dressed-up our bodies, would that we have not forgotten our immortal souls, but bethought ourselves of the great promise, namely that we shall renounce the devil and all his works and all his ways and believe in the Triune God, Father, Son, and Holy Spirit."

His greatest spiritual danger was to become so absorbed in the concerns of the world as to lose his soul; for he had unusual talent in several directions. He was for a time an assistant to his brother who was bailiff of the district. He busied himself with carpentry, blacksmithing, bee-culture, clearing of a piece of land, and also engaged in trading in a small way.

His final awakening came when in 1795 he became a store clerk in the city of Fredriksstad. At home the world had been at a distance, as a thing to seek or not to seek. In the city he was placed in the midst of ungodly, frivolous, sensual surroundings, where he was compelled to choose whether God or the world should have his allegiance. In a moment of weakness he indulged too freely in the use of liquor, became intoxicated, and felt so humiliated that for a while he did not know what to do. At the same time, his companions made fun of his constant reading of religious books, telling him that if he kept on like that, he would become insane. But terrible as the struggle was, he won the day. The world might tempt him, but it could not win him. He was pledged to the service of his Lord. Evidently at the request of his parents he returned to his home, read the Bible and other religious books, prayed for the Holy Spirit, spoke to others about their soul's salvation, and met their opposition with searching still deeper for the foundation on which he might build his faith.

Thus Hauge was gradually carried forward to the day when he should become fully conscious of the two things that were to be the controlling factors in shaping his destiny: His own full assurance of the grace of God, and an irrepressible, irresistible desire to save others.

Hauge was not converted suddenly. Yet a sudden transformation did take place in his inner life. His struggle had not been that between faith and doubt, but that between willingness and unwillingness to follow God's call. And this long and gradual development shaped his whole future life, made him independent of men in his conception of the Christian doctrine, in his way of presenting the gospel for the acceptance or rejection of men, and caused him to lay particular stress on faith as a power unto regeneration as well as on the duty of a true believer on the one hand not to commit idolatry with created things and on the other hand to be diligent and faithful in the performance of one's daily duties. He was the disciple of no man. He had been taught of God. As his appearance was extraordinary, so was his awakening unusual.

* * *

Hauge was two days past his twenty-fifth year when, on the fifth of April, 1796, he was out working in the field on his father's farm. It was a beautiful spring-day. The very weather was Pentecostal. Trees were budding, birds were singing, flowers were beginning to bloom.

As Hauge was doing his work, he was singing what evidently was one of his favorite hymns, as it has been a favorite hymn with all who have had a similar experience:

"Jesus, I long for Thy blessed communion."

Then, as he was singing the second verse:

"Mightily strengthen my spirit within me,
    That I may learn what Thy Spirit can do!
O take Thou captive each passion within me,
    Lead Thou and guide me my whole journey through!
All that I am and possess I surrender,
    If Thou alone in my spirit mayst dwell,
All will I yield Thee, my Savior most tender.
    Take me and own me, and all will be well,"—

he seemed to be lifted up from earth, and his soul was filled with the peace "that passeth all understanding."

This is rightly called Hauge's spiritual, his pentecostal baptism.

And in answer to his prayer, "Lord, what wilt Thou that I should do," he was reminded of what the prophet Isaiah had said:

47

"Here I am, Lord. Send me." Deep within him he heard a voice, saying: "Thou shalt confess my name before men, exhort them to repent and seek Me while I am to be found, to call upon Me while I am near, to touch their hearts, so that they may pass over from darkness to light."

This is neither "emotion," nor "fanaticism," nor "mysticism," but the way in which God deals with men whom he has chosen to do a special work in His Kingdom.

And Hauge was one of these.

Can anyone at all conversant with similar spiritual experiences (of which there are many, thank God!), understand how a Lutheran pastor could place Hauge's experience in the class of "a sort of magnetic clairvoyance?" As a result of this experience, Hauge saw, as he had never seen it before, the world steeped in sin and lost in iniquity. In his book, "The Christian Doctrine," published in Copenhagen in 1800, he describes just what he saw. And still people wondered why he (who knew that he himself was saved and saw an unsaved world of men and women all around him), could not keep still!

The above-mentioned book not only justifies Hauge's work, but gives a picture of the life of his own day, which explains why he was received as he was. In order fully to understand the difficulties with which Hauge had to cope, one must read this book.

It was a "mirror of the times" such as no other man at that time produced.

It will also make it perfectly clear that Hauge's mission could be no other than that of preaching repentance and conversion. He never wanted to found a new church, nor to reform the doctrinal system of the church, nor to make any change in its worship or policy or outward organization. These things did not concern him. What did concern him was to see to it that men were brought to God. And for this work God had bestowed upon him special qualifications. Did ever man live in Norway who could speak to his fellow-men as could Hauge? "Besides," says Hauge's biographer, Dr. Theol., Bishop A. Chr. Bang, "in respect to spiritual gifts and personal independence, Hauge ranks as the equal to any man of his own day."

But what right had he to do this? The question has been asked many times and answered in various ways. Today we may quite properly ask another question: What right had anyone to prevent Hauge from doing what he did? What right has anyone to prevent any man whom God has called from preaching the gospel?

To a churchly as well as civilly loyal man like Hauge it became necessary to make his position clear to himself. He did not rush headlong into the work. He weighed and examined and considered, and when he had arrived at a full conviction of his scriptural right to preach, he never wavered, but stood like a rock.

In connection with the question of a layman's right to preach the gospel, it is of more than academic interest to note that just one hundred years before Hauge began to preach, Paschasius Quesnel (Ke'nel), a Roman Catholic Father of the famous Jansenist Society of Port Royal, near Paris, wrote and published a New Testament commentary, in which he promulgates as good Christian doctrine that laymen, and even women, have the right and are under obligation to edify themselves and instruct others through the reading of Holy Scripture. The Pope, of course, condemned such teaching.

We as Lutherans pride ourselves on the firm stand which Luther took at Worms. Yet even Luther was permitted to defend himself, to give cogent and scriptural reasons for what he taught and did. He was not condemned unheard. Time and again he was permitted to defend himself before individuals and large convocations, till he was finally permitted to stand before the Emperor and the representatives of the Holy Roman Empire and the high dignitaries of the Church of Rome and lay before the whole Diet his reasons for not being able to recant his opinions. But who ever heard of the civil or the ecclesiastical authorities of Norway or Denmark suggesting that Hauge be permitted to lay his case before a representative gathering of church officials.

Yet the martyrs of the early Christian Church were not condemned before they had been given an opportunity to bring a proper defense before a Roman tribunal, although—in those days of a pagan government—to be a Christian was tantamount to "crimen majestatis." It would be difficult to find in history a more defenseless and high-handed procedure than that which laid Hauge in chains.

How did Hauge himself look upon this matter?

As a converted man he felt justified in obeying the Lord's command to Peter: "When thou art converted, strengthen thy brethren." (Luke 22, 32). He understood Christ to have commanded him to do the very thing he did in Matt. 21, 16, as well as in Luke 9,50 and 19,40.

The civil authorities found many reasons for forbidding Hauge to preach, chiefly this, that he was not called by them. Was the Church, then, established by civil authority?

But the ultimate justification of Hauge's preaching rests on the undisputed fact that as a general rule the clergy of Norway in his day did not preach the gospel, but instead, proclaimed their own unscriptural rationalistic conceits, encouraged in this by the very civil government that sentenced Hauge. That alone is sufficient to condemn any state-church. We shall now follow Hauge.

This assurance that he was really a child of God filled his soul with an exquisite joy, and his first thought was to tell his parents, his brothers and sisters about it.

Being afraid that he might be misunderstood, he restrained himself till in the evening, when he spoke to his sisters, two of whom he won that very night. The first fruits of his work was a younger sister, Anne, who is spoken of as a true Mary sitting at the feet of Jesus.

During the three weeks which followed upon his full and conscious conversion, he experienced an undisturbed peace and calm of soul, and the things of the world in which he had hitherto shown so much interest became so repulsive to him that he was in danger of forgetting the injunction of the Savior: to be a faithful householder also in temporal things. But the Word of God, which he read day and night, sleeping only a couple of hours and taking very little nourishment, finally showed him the right way.

His mother was at first in deep grief at the change which had taken place, and actually went so far as to beg him to desist. This motherly anxiety was due to the fact that she thought her dear son was becoming insane. One of the most touching points in Hauge's life is the way in which he, the son, tenderly but firmly told her that he could not turn back, and that she must try to come to the same way. In short, the whole family of nine were, like the Christians of Jerusalem, of one mind, daily praising

51

God, offering up true sacrifices on the altar of faith morning and evening.

The home of Nils Mikkelsen and Marie Olsdaughter (for these were the names of the parents) became the center of a movement that was destined to spread far and wide, and out of this home walked one day the man on whom God had laid His hand and said: "Go, and I will be with thee."

One would like to have been near when the father, perhaps while talking with a neighbor who came to express concern as to how this was going to end up, said in his calm, confident way: "Oh, Hans will manage it all right."

These first weeks after the great change was the calm before the storm. For it was not very long after this that his intellect started to bother him with rationalistic questions concerning "election." He was unable to see how God could deliberately harden men's hearts so that they would be lost, and at the same time tell him to go and preach the gospel of salvation. Was not this worse than nonsense? Was it not a mockery on God's part? And what good would his preaching do if God saved whom He chose and hardened whom He chose?

A violent struggle went on within him, till he became physically exhausted and fell asleep. When he woke up, he was more calm, and after he had prayed for light in this terrible darkness he received an answer in the words of Paul: "God wants all men to be saved and come to the knowledge of truth." Furthermore, he came to see that God does not take His Holy Spirit away from any soul until that soul has hardened itself against God. No man can be saved against his will.

Then there came the struggle between the cravings of the flesh and the yearnings of the spirit for purity in the inmost heart, and for a whole night he prayed, asking in childlike simplicity if God would not take these evil desires away from him.

"How can I serve Thee and confess Thy name to others, when I, myself, am so beset with impure thoughts," he said. Also in this he received the answer to his prayer from Paul: "The strength of God is made perfect through weakness."

He found that this daily struggle was necessary in order to keep him humble before God and man. And often later he, too, experienced the wonderful blessing of being able to help others in their temptations because he himself had been tempted.

Thus was Hauge prepared for his work in the only true scriptural way: Seeking always in the Word of God for an answer to his questionings, and being able to lead others into peace with God because he himself had experienced that peace.

Did Hauge begin to preach publicly as soon as he was sure of his own salvation and had heard the call of God to become a messenger? No, he did not. Altogether, there is such exquisite reticence, such sublime tact in the behavior of Hauge, that it is passing strange how anyone, even in that rationalistic day, could take offense.

The whole summer through he spoke to individuals only, thus gaining that wonderful insight into the condition of particular souls which afterwards became, shall we say, the most outstanding "feature" of his method in winning souls. Unconsciously, perhaps, he was pursuing the only psychological course that would make him an expert soul-winner, which also accounts for his all but irresistible power as well as for the lasting devotion of his followers. And when he did appear in public, it was not in the spirit of a firey revivalist, as is so often the case with young converts, but with fear and trembling.

Some there were that heard him gladly, while others accused him of hypocrisy and pharisaism, and said that he and those he converted would land in bedlam.

Some said that Hauge worshipped mysterious beings and that he taught people to jump down from the roofs of houses in order that their faith might be put to a test.

Then again there was a terrible temptation in the expressed wish of some that they might become like him, and it required all his spiritual strength to meet this temptation, which has ruined so many gifted men. This he did so effectually at the very beginning that it does not seem to have caused him a great deal of difficulty after that.

But while he experienced great joy when someone showed signs of a sincere repentance, the overwhelming wickedness of his surroundings made him falter, and he actually arrived at a point where he asked God to release him from his work, to send a bishop or some other great man in his place. He, himself, would rather die. Then God answered him in the only convincing way for a deep soul like that of Hauge: "Do you wish to die now? You have formerly served sin. Will you not now, when you are saved, bring Me some fruit of My work in you? You have promised to serve Me. Have I not often used the lowly in this world, called them from the plow, used shepherds and cowherds, fishermen and publicans?

"I will give you wisdom and strength, which your enemies shall not be able to withstand. Be firm in your purpose and continue in patience."

In this way he was led to see that God had called him to be a servant who was to speak whether they would hear him or not. It was God's work he was to do, not his own.

Thus he found peace once more.

There is an admirable sequence in the steps of Hauge's public appearance as a speaker. He had won his own folks first of all; he then spoke to individuals whom he met casually; his first public utterance was at a meeting in his own home, because there had been created a desire to hear the Word of God. The Holy Spirit was plowing up the soil. Hauge followed and threw the seed into the furrows. Finally there came the day when he stepped outside of the family circle and delivered his first message at the home of Iver Graalum in Tune. This meeting is characteristic. At all his former meetings, Hauge had invited the parish minister, the Rev. Stevelin Urdal, to be present. But he had never done so, though the Conventicle Act stated specifically that this was the minister's duty. Thus it was not Hauge, but the clergyman of his parish, who disregarded the law which Hauge was accused of violating. This time the minister came, and with him his curate and the sub-prefect or magistrate of the district, Radich, who was to gain an unenviable reputation as a blind persecutor of the gospel.

These three sat through the meeting. When Hauge had finished, the parish minister arose and forbade him to hold any more meetings. Hauge retorted quietly that he did not think anyone had any right to forbid him to exhort people to repent and believe, as long as he did this in conformity with the Word of God. Then he asked the minister if anything he had said was contrary to the Word of God, or the Lutheran Confession of Faith?

To this question Hauge received no answer. Instead, the minister asked the magistrate to let the

55

people know what the law decreed. Mr. Radich said that the Conventicle Act of 1741 forbade such meetings.

Hauge was of a different opinion, said he had the Conventicle Act with him, and asked permission to have it read, so the people could judge as to what it permitted and what it did not permit. But the minister and the magistrate said it was their business to give the people such information and would not permit the reading of the Act. This angered the audience, and several asked if it was the purpose of the authorities to hinder that which was good. The meetings had been held in strict conformity with the law, many had changed to a better way of living, drunkenness and other vices had become less prevalent—altogether the meetings had exerted a good influence. If the authorities permitted gatherings where drunkenness, brawls, and many other indecencies were committed, so that the public order was constantly disturbed, what sense was there in forbidding meetings where people came together to sing hymns, pray, and listen to the Word of God?

Neither these officers, nor others to whom the same questions were repeated again and again all over Norway, could have anything to say to this. The logic of the common man has a peculiar faculty of cutting through all legal quibbles.

Some days later Hauge was invited to the parsonage and asked to let the minister have a written copy of his address at the Graalum farm. When he had received it, he sent it, together with his own report of what had taken place at the Graalum farm, to the bishop at Christiania.

In his report the parish minister describes Hauge as a fanatic, his adherents as "enthusiasts" and the whole movement as an evil which should be crushed right in its beginning. But the bishop had more sense than the minister, which fortunately was often the case, and it should be said in justice to the then bishops of Norway as well as to the highest functionaries, that they were more tolerant than the common clergy and the lower functionaries, who often seem to have lost all sense and reason and to have acted as if Hauge was a wild beast or a dangerous criminal.

At the ordination of Lutheran ministers, the candidate reads, or some one else reads it for him, what is called his "vita," i. e., a brief autobiography, in order that the public may know who he is and how and why he has arrived at the decision of becoming a servant of the Word. Something like this may have been in Hauge's mind when in the summer of 1796 he set to work to write his first book, in which he tells how he himself had obtained peace with God. He felt called upon to do this on account of the many untruthful rumors circulated about him.

This little pamphlet was bound together with the book which Hauge wrote right after with the title, "The Foolishness of the World." By "foolishness" he means the true faith, which Paul says is "foolishness to the world."

Here we have Hauge's programme. With these two manuscripts Hauge sets out on foot for Christiana, now Oslo, to find a publisher. The distance was between 60 and 70 miles. But he had only proceeded about ten miles when he missed his manuscripts. Then he wondered whether this was a "pointer" from God that he was not to publish the books.

He actually felt relieved, and started up a by-way to visit an acquaintance. After a while another traveler arrived and said he had found some papers on the road. This proved to be the missing manuscripts. So Hauge sets off once more. After he had proceeded a distance on his way he felt an urgent call to pray God for His blessing, and that He would protect him in all dangers and keep him through all temptations. While Hauge was praying, a man approached him unobserved and stood listening till Hauge had finished, when the man came up to him and asked if he was ill. Hauge answered him that his body was healthy, but his soul might not have the strength and health he could desire it to have. This led the stranger to believe that Hauge, whom he did not know, was out of his mind. And when Hauge continued to speak to him about spiritual matters, his only answer was: "You are crazy, you should not go about alone." Hauge now understood that the man was utterly ignorant in spiritual matters, so he at once turned the conversation into other channels, spoke about his farming, advised him to try a new method, gained the man's confidence so that he walked six miles past his place in order to get this other "new information" about his soul which needs just as careful a cultivation as the land, if anything good is to come from it, and when Hauge parted with him this man, who had been living an immoral life, was already in the Kingdom, so that many wondered what had happened to him.

He had met Hauge, and through him he found Christ.

As Hauge came near enough to the Capital so that he could see the towers and the houses, he again was attacked by doubt. What business had he, a poor farmer-boy, to print books, especially one in which he censured the clergy and took them to task for their worldliness and lack of spirituality? They would no sooner see his manuscript than they would report him to the bishop, and then he would be put in jail.

Even today, with all our vaunted liberty, a young man of tender conscience might hesitate before he gave publicity to such a book.

We must bear in mind that this was at a time when there was no such a thing as liberty of conscience, when an absolutistic government put men in prison and kept them there without trial, sometimes for life, confiscated property without due process of law, and did anything it felt inclined to do, regardless of justice or mercy. It will be remembered that when the Bastille of Paris was stormed in the French Revolution, an Englishman was found who did not know why he was put there. For years, an entirely unknown man was kept a prisoner in the fortress of Akershus in Christiania (now Oslo). He died there. The temptation was crucial, momentous, fateful. Suppose he had yielded to his fears, turned back and became a farmer as before, kept silence, become like the rest!

Soul-murdering thoughts arose in him. "There is neither a heaven nor a hell. Man has no immortal soul. The Word of God is all a lie." And a voice behind him seemed to say, "Turn about, turn about, and go home."

Still he kept going, and with fear and trembling he asked the way to a printer's. Not till the third day was he able to make arrangements for the publication of his two little books, the manuscripts of which, together with thirteen dollars,—all the cash money he had in his pocket—he deposited with Jens Oerbek Berg, the printer and publisher. As the French say, "It is the first step that counts." In later years Hauge understood that the Evil One was trying so hard to prevent the publication of his first little book just because it was to be the means of turning many hearts to God.

All over Norway there were souls "in bondage," in a spiritual prison. Young men and women had no one from whom they could receive guidance in their spiritual difficulties. Parents were afraid that they were going insane. The minister spoke about "fanaticism" and counselled "blood-letting" as a cure for the disease. Relatives advised that they should throw themselves into a whirl of amusements so as to get rid of these serious thoughts. Then this little book would come, singing like a little bird about peace and joy and salvation.

A young farmer-boy down in Smaalenene was telling of his experience to thousands. Night became day. Clouds vanished. Souls were set free. No wonder, when this young man came walking quietly along the road, singing as he went, they would flock around him, listen to his talk, and ever after look upon him as one who had led them out of bondage into the glorious liberty of the children of God.

The publication of these little books was the modest beginning of that vast stream of Christian literature that has since filled Norway with thoughts of things divine.

The old devotional literature was still extant, as we have seen. Hauge himself was nurtured by it. But the most gifted of Norway's ministers published books that contained everything else except what could lead the souls to Christ and His Cross. Some of them were excellent books in their way, learned and useful, but materialistic and rationalistic. Surely, if Christianity was not to disappear entirely, it was high time someone, no matter in how crude a way, told people something that might awaken in them thoughts of God and eternity, and also remind them that no one comes to the Father except through the Son.

In addition to these two books, Hauge at the same time published an old Danish translation from German (author unknown) of a book that bears the title: "Evangelical Rules of Life," to which he added a brief explanation of the "Lord's Prayer" which he himself composed.

These "Rules of Life" are interesting, on the one hand because they show us what Hauge thought a Christian life ought to be, and on the other hand because nothing better has ever been published on the subject. Rendered into our language we should say that it was a book quite up-to-date. Just a few brief extracts to prove its worth:

"1. Let nothing in the world entice you away from (a) the Word of God, (b) the faith in Christ, (c) true godliness. Let Holy Writ be the only rule for your faith and for your life. If you read other religious books, then prove them carefully according to God's Word; but let no book of man lead you away from your faith in Christ Jesus.

Believe on Jesus (that you would love Him and follow in His steps), then you will obtain salvation by grace through His merits. Strive after sanctification, so that you may leave off evil and grow in all that which is good.

2. For exercise in true godliness (a) pray, (b) read the Word of God, (c) examine yourself, your faults and weaknesses. Pray diligently and ask God for His Holy Spirit, which God gives only to those who make earnest of their struggle against sin. Set aside part of each day for communion with God in prayer. Do not forget to pray for all men, friends and enemies, and the whole of Christendom.

Every morning take a verse of Holy Writ for comfort and strength during the day. Every evening, before you retire, make up your account with God. If you have done something that is good, thank God humbly for it. If you have done something that is evil, ask God for a full pardon for Christ's sake.

If God has laid a good foundation in your heart, then do not be ashamed to confess it before men. Rejoice if the world does not honor you, but considers you foolish and hypocritical, and reviles you; but do not yield a hair's breadth from the true path.

Be a pattern to others in humility, kindliness, sincere charity, patience, and courtesy.

Wherever an opportunity offers itself, be kind and helpful to the poor, the sick, to those in distress. This is being Christ-minded.

Judge not lightly anyone, for we judge a hundred times and perhaps judge rightly but once.

What you do not understand, leave it to God, who gives understanding to those that are simple-minded."

These sentences are as if spoken from the heart of Hauge. He lived his life in constant and faithful practice of them.

Having arranged for the printing of these books, Hauge again started for home, and peculiarly enough he was again beset with questionings. As if the very air of the capital had contaminated him, he began, while walking along the road, to ponder on eternity, the immortality of the soul, and the nature of God. To regain his composure, he left the road and sought a few hours' sleep under the trees. When he awoke, he promised himself never again to permit his natural reason to busy itself with these problems, and ever after he warned his friends against these useless speculations. "God," he told them, "would not be the supernatural Being He is, and eternity would not be

62

an object of faith, if our natural reason could comprehend these things."

Was this unlearned farmer-boy from Tune right or wrong in this? Could a learned man express it any better?

During the summer of 1796, Hauge was busy on the farm, studied the Bible, held meetings, and wrote a new book on "God's Wisdom."

One interesting phase of this new work is that the author in it predicts the coming of a better day for Christianity. He feels sure that a change is coming.

By the end of September he is again in Christiania, where he remained three months, learning to print and bind books.

This time he must have become well acquainted in the capital city. It would be interesting to give a sketch of life as it was lived there at this time—the end of the eighteenth century. Space does not permit this. But one observation seems pertinent.

As the unpretentious farmer-boy walked to and fro in the city which at that time had but eleven thousand inhabitants or so, he may have met (of course, without knowing it) the man who was Norway's first philosopher. His name was Niels Treschow, who was then principal of the High School. As the name indicates, the family descended from a Danish maker of wooden shoes. Many names of equally famous families indicate an equally humble origin. Professor Treschow was a very learned man. This very winter of 1796-1797 he delivered a course of lectures on the great German philosopher, Immanuel Kant. Treschow's criticism of Kant's "theory of cognition," now usually called "epistemology," or "theory of knowledge," became famous. In fact, it is much nearer the present day philosophy than is that of Kant. Needless to say that the "elite" of Christiania attended these lectures.

63

Treschow was in Christiania from 1789 to 1803, when he was called to the Copenhagen university, where he occupied the chair of philosophy from 1803 to 1813.

In 1806-1807, when Hauge had begun to serve his sentence in the city prison of Christiania for having preached the Word of God, Treschow delivered philosophical lectures in Copenhagen. In these he developed what is now called "the theory of evolution" based on biological ground, holding that man is a link in the series of organic beings, and he outlines, years in advance of the famous Englishman, Charles Darwin, the origin of species. Life he said, has its roots in the sea, gaining more and more perfect forms, until finally man arrives on the scene.

Naturally, Treschow had to "assume" some ancestor for this new and more perfect type of species, and he arrives at the conclusion that man is descended either from the sea-cow (walrus), or from some species of ape. It is generally admitted that this Norwegian philosopher was the first to present this theory in the learned world.

Now, let us stop for just a moment to consider this matter. The philosopher, Niels Treschow, who denies that man was created in the image of God, is not only made professor of philosophy at the University of Copenhagen, but when a university was founded at Christiania, in 1811, is made its professor of philosophy, its chancellor, and a counsellor of state after 1814, while Hans Nielsen Hauge, who preached the pure gospel of Christ to the common people of Norway is put in prison for it at the same time.

Not a voice of bishop or minister or government is raised against the monkey-theory of Treschow, while the whole machinery of Church and State is put in operation to crush Hauge.

Is there not here food for reflection?

The irony of it all becomes apparent when Halvdan Koht, in his great work, "Our Leaders," in which he has gathered the pictures and biographies of Norway's greatest men, lets the article on Hauge follow immediately after that of Treschow. Now, suppose these two men had met in Christiania in 1796 (for both were there near Christmas in that year) and the question had been raised: Which of these two, the learned philosopher and the unlearned farmer-boy, will benefit his country most and be remembered longest, what would the cultured upper class of Christiania have said?

Yet today it is a perfectly safe statement to make that where hundreds remember Treschow, thousands remember, love, and honor Hauge.

Again we say: God works in a mysterious way His wonders to perform.

The year 1796 is drawing to a close. Hauge is again at home during the Christmas season, binding his little books, preaching, and preparing himself for his bigger tasks.

The new day is beginning to dawn.

# COVERING NORWAY ON FOOT

## SECOND PERIOD, 1797-1804

During this, the second period of his life, Hauge traveled through Norway from one end to another.

As we follow him on his travels, we must bear in mind the physical features of Norway: its rugged, mountainous character, its deep valleys, its stately forests, its rivers and waterfalls, its countless islands and beautiful but dangerous fjords. Also that this was in the last years of the eighteenth and the first years of the nineteenth century, with few wagon roads, let alone highways or railroads, with no steamers, no telegraph, very few hotels, and those only in the largest cities.

Yet, to follow Hauge and his co-workers in their journeys is to visit every city, every rural district, every upland valley—to cross mountains, to sail fjords, to follow rivers, to pass through forests, to cover the whole country from Fredrikshald and Lindesnes to Tromsoe, and from Bergen and Stat to Roeraas,—an achievement as marvelous as it was blessed. And for this sole purpose: to carry the Word of God into every home, every nook and corner of the land.

Talk about home mission work! Miles and miles of travel in midwinter over untrodden snowfields, sleeping in the snow at night north of the Polar Circle, living for days on nothing but "bark-bread," denied shelter and food; carrying on their back big packages of books for free distribution; haunted and hunted like criminals from place to place, often imprisoned for days at the caprice of some officious bailiff; harassed in every way; and all the time singing, praying, preaching, and comforting and encouraging the little gatherings of people that came to listen to the young lay-preacher from Smaalenene, or his fellow-workers! Oh, the Christian love and patience and courage and blessing of it all!

This great work was begun by Hauge in 1797, and ended at the city jail in Christiania in 1804, after eight years of incessant activity.

Between January and June 1797, Hauge visited nearly all the parishes between his own home and Christiania, preaching in Fredriksstad, Moss, Christiania and Drammen.

In the city of Moss, the minister, Rev. Hans H. Thaulow, was an out and out rationalist, without any understanding of what Christianity meant. Desirous to know what kind of a man Hauge was, he attended a Sunday afternoon meeting. It should be noticed that Hauge never held meetings during the hours of regular church service, and always went to church himself, regardless of the person who happened to be the officiating pastor.

"The services," says Thaulow, "consisted in this, that two persons in the audience sang a few verses of a hymn, after which Hauge spoke. That was all." Rev. Thaulow, in a magazine article, says that the whole thing appeared to him as "devotional nonsense"; the talk "the most miserable wishy-washy stuff," so that he could barely "refrain from laughing aloud," and he told the people assembled that as far as he was concerned they could go on all they pleased, just so they did not keep people from their work on week days. Later on, when this "miserable stuff" caused many to wake up, when a new life grew out of these meetings, he became one of Hauge's bitterest opponents and detractors.

From Moss, Hauge walked to Christiania.

The then bishop of the diocese was the 71 year old Christian Schmidt, who had been a "great orator" in his younger days, but now was without any spiritual power. He hoped that this "enthusiasm" would die out. But when he saw the movement grow stronger and stronger till it threatened to destroy the old fabric of things, he became frightened, and the formerly tolerant bishop became a violent opponent. With the exception of one, the ministers of Christiania were all rationalists, the exception being the dean Nikolai Lumholtz, who was very friendly to Hauge, and, when his son became Hauge's attorney, helped him to write up the defense in 1813.

Of the others, Pihl and Herlofsen resigned from the ministry, the first even tried his hand as "circus-rider," and Herlofsen in 1809 became a business man in Larvik. Ole R. Sandberg, Johan Keyser, and Fredrik Schmidt were outspoken rationalists. Keyser, whose father was a merchant in Drammen by the name of Christian Nielsen, later became bishop in Christianssand, a kindly and humane man, much beloved for his tolerance, but as bishop too sickly to be able to do much. Keyser's daughter married a certain "head-master" Preus, and their son was the well-known Rev. H. A. Preus, one of the founders and most prominent ministers of the Norwegian Synod of America. These were the men who were to be "shepherds" in the capital of Norway, where life was godless and worldly to an almost incredible degree. Their Christian influence was practically nil.

In Christiania, Hauge found a few "crippled" remnants of an earlier Moravian (Herrnhutian) revival.

In Aker he found not a few, and they became his friends. The revival in Aker dated from the time of the Rev. Johannes Green, who as pastor both in Fron,

Gudbrandsdalen, and in Aker (he also became palace preacher), held devotional meetings in his house. This greatly "offended" the bishop Niels Dorph, a strictly orthodox man, "who," says Bishop Dr. Bang, "was one of those that put doctrine before life, the letter above the spirit, strain the gnat and swallow the camel.'

During a visitation at Noetteroe in 1839, this Norwegian Lutheran bishop was greatly shocked by a sermon, in which the Rev. Hartvig stated that "we are poor sinners, in ourselves lost and condemned." In Larvik he received another severe shock when he heard the curate, Ole Tidemand, later bishop in Bergen and Christianssand, teach the catechumens that the first work of the Holy Spirit was to "call" men, while the bishop held the view that the "Church" was the first work of the Spirit. The people of the day were more shocked, however, at the "unorthodox life" of this bishop. Since Dr. Bang does not mention the bishop's lapses from orthodox living, we shall not do so either.

While Hauge was always glad to find true believers, he often found it impossible to associate himself with the Moravians.

Strange, wasn't it! They were Christians, and so was he. Why, then, could he not unite himself with them?

These Moravians were followers of the famous Count Zinzendorf, whose Christ-like life has been an inspiration to many. But just as little as all Christians are like Christ, or all Lutherans like Luther, just so little were all Moravians like Zinzendorf, and some of their peculiarities grated on the religious nerves of so soundly and profoundly scriptural and Lutheran a man as Hauge.

So Lutheran was Hauge that his Lutheranism was

the very reason why the rationalistic ministers of his day persecuted him. It is an established fact that the large majority of Norway's bishops and ministers in Hauge's day were "false teachers." They, and not he, should have been forbidden to preach. If the Church of Norway and Denmark had been in reality what it was in name, it should have deposed nearly all its bishops and the large majority of its ministers, made Hauge a bishop, and some of his co-workers ministers. That would have been logical, scriptural, and merciful. What Hauge and his friends lacked in theological learning would have been more than balanced by what they possessed of biblical knowledge, evangelical zeal, pure life, and willingness to sacrifice themselves and all they had in the service of the Lord. In fact, if not in name, Hans Nielsen Hauge was Norway's universal bishop during these eight years of splendid activity. He not only knew his Bible, and preached its truths whether it pleased men or not; he not only had the unction of the Spirit in an unusual degree, as is clearly evidenced by his blameless life and his wonderful success; but he preached incessantly, in season and out of season, and carried the gospel through the length and breadth of the land, suffered with Christian patience every humiliation, and sacrificed himself and all he had for the sake of the Word of God; and while imprisoned, prayed for the Church and his enemies, that God would bring them to repentance and salvation. What more could a bishop do?

It is just as right to call Hauge Norway's unanointed bishop as it is to call Bjørnson Norway's uncrowned king.

But he could not work together with the Herrnhutians, because they laid too one-sided stress on Christ's redemptory work, and almost entirely overlooked the first and the third article of our Christian creed.

Some of them were, no doubt, warm-hearted Christians; and it shall be said to their honor, that in a time of great laxity they lifted high "the cross on which Christ died for sinners." On the other hand, too many of them were not very earnest in their work of sanctification. Some of them even went so far as to say, in act, if not in words, that since all sins are forgiven, it does not matter if we sin—and some of them sinned grievously.

Emotional Christianity often bears this bitter fruit of moral laxness.

It is historically correct, as Dr. Bang says, that on account of their errors, the Herrnhutians, instead of being a bulwark against rationalism, when it broke in full force during the latter half of the eighteenth century, actually prepared the way for it; and some of the Herrnhutians, bishops, ministers, and people, became the most outspoken rationalists. We are experiencing the same among the Reformed churches in America today. Naturally enough, they in turn accused Hauge of being a "legalist," even a pharisee.

It goes without saying that Hauge could establish no relation of friendship with the anabaptistic "Zionites" in Aker and Lier, near Drammen, though there were true Christians among them, and some of them returned to "the Church of their fathers."

Returning home from Drammen, where the Herrnhutians had been warned against him and would have nothing to do with him, he took up farm labor, and preached in various places.

A visitation was held on June 27, 1797, by the dean Johannes Henrik Berg, perhaps one of the rankest rationalists in Norway at that time.

Hauge, who wished to testify, placed himself among the young people on the "floor."

Two reports are preserved of this visitation, one by the Rev. Mr. Berg, the other by T. O. Bache, a friend of Hauge.

The dean says that Hauge "stood there with his "gloomy" face (another adjective used by the reverent gentleman is not fit to print), and was utterly ignorant even of the fundamentals of religion and morals," i. e., he means rationalism.

Bache, on the other hand, says that Hauge answered when the other boys were unable to do so, and answered all the questions put to him directly, to the satisfaction of the dean. The truth of the matter seems to be this, that the dean examined Hauge a long time, not knowing that it was he. When he finally discovered whom he had been examining, he said that each one should answer for himself—and left the rest of the examination to the Rev. Urdal, who though no friend of Hauge, and moreover the first man who struck Hauge, declared publicly, that Hauge's answers at this examination were completely satisfactory.

During the summer (1797) Hauge again set out on a longer journey, across the water to Holmestrand, through the "counties" of Jarlsberg and Larvik, to Toensberg, Vaale, and Drammen. In the latter place he now held his first meeting in the house of the merchant Mads Moeller, a gifted and independent man, whose fundamental principle of a Christian life is found in the words of Christ: "The truth shall make you free," and in the words of Paul: "Where the Spirit of Christ is, there is liberty." In a letter written some years later, this splendid type of a Christian layman expresses the wish "that the Lord may give to many the courage to preach the Word, regardless of what the world may say or do, as we know that it behooves us through much tribulation to enter into the Kingdom of God. But the way to this spiritual freedom is through self-denial and prayer, that God may give us strength to become freed from all that hinders our growth in grace."

In mentioning this letter, Dr. Bang calls attention to the fact that "while the mighty spirit of Hauge is noticeable in the lives of all his faithful adherents, yet they all possess a peculiar independence of mind, the foundation of which is to seek in a spiritual sobriety which did not permit them to take any positive stand in advance of what they had experienced spiritually."

This, again, is to be accounted for by Hauge's truly apostolic exhortation to his friends: Follow Christ! Hauge never said, Follow me.

Incidentally we may say here that the only lay delegates at Eidsvold in 1814, who were able to speak their minds freely, were friends of Hauge. No wonder Norway's official publication for the Paris Exposition in 1900, in its article on "Literature," page 495, has this to say:

"The political emancipation (of 1814) was accompanied by a regeneration of the religious life among the people in a revival that was led by the "Peasant Apostle," Hans Nielsen Hauge."

He himself had said: "They may not understand me now; but some day they will know that a prophet has been among them." If anyone thinks this extravagant, we shall let them know that Bishop Bang calls the laymen's activity a "prophetic" as against "priestly" activity.

From Drammen Hauge travelled to Kongsberg, where the minister, Cornelius Norman, was a spiritual man whom Hauge must have found joy in meeting.

Hauge then returned home again; but both on his way to Kongsberg and upon his return, he visited at

Eker, where the soil was thus prepared for the great revival which came later on, one of the finest fruits of Hauge's work.

Barring a few visits to Fredriksstad and one visit to Fredrikshald, Hauge remained quietly at home till Christmas, 1797.

The question may now be asked: Why did not Hauge start at once on a country-wide evangelistic campaign? The correct answer is no doubt that given by Steenerson in his book about Hauge: He did not think himself strong enough to become a national revivalist. This is characteristic of the whole attitude of Hauge. The Lord was leading him step by step, and Hauge was following in the footsteps of all true followers of the Lord. Rashness and foolhardiness were as far from Hauge as were carnal calculations and cowardice. He never conferred with "flesh and blood."

———

At this time there is another turning point in the life of Hauge. He happened upon the well-known story of the conversion of Johan Tauler. This learned doctor of theology and Dominican friar of Strassburg was led to a true conversion by a Waldensian layman, Nicolaus of Basel. Upon the advice of the layman, the learned doctor ceased to preach till be had found peace with God. When this point in the spiritual development of Tauler was reached, the layman said to him: "Now you can preach." And he added: "From now on, after you have had the experience of conversion and grace, one sermon will bear more fruit than formerly a hundred sermons. Tauler found it so to his great joy. The sermons of Tauler made a profound impression on Hauge. They fitted his case admirably, especially the gripping story of how, after his conversion, Tauler said that "a faithful and honest

74

bride is in duty bound to shun all that is contrary to her bridegroom's wishes."

Hauge, though a layman, became confirmed in his spiritual right to preach the gospel. As the layman Nicolaus of Basel was the means of converting the learned but spiritually dead doctor of theology, so Hauge would go out and preach conversion to the spiritually dead people of Norway. He had received the call to be an evangelist. He would leave the official pastoral duties of administering the sacraments as well as the public preaching of the Word in the churches to the regularly ordained clergy. He never encroached upon their duties. What he claimed as his particular right was one which neither king nor bishop nor minister nor prefect could deprive him of: to preach the gospel to the people he met, gather them on Sunday afternoons, or week day evenings, and speak to them about the salvation of their souls.

Now, while Hauge himself was the soul of the movement started by him, he was not to do his work alone. And as he himself was from Smaalenene, so his first messengers are called "the teachers from Smaalenene," which thus—with reverence be it said— became a sort of "Galilee of Norway." They were not all of them of the same calibre as Hauge, they did not all possess the same amount of wisdom, power, and strength of will, or the gift of the Spirit in the same degree, but they were all spiritual men, worthy to be the co-workers of Hauge. To notice where they all came from and where they went is to "pinhead" Norway all over. Thus a veritable gospel net was spread over the beautiful country. Spiritual colonies were established, till there were very few who had not heard the Word, or could have heard it, if they had so desired, from these missionaries of Christ. Perhaps no land save Palestine, ever had such a day of visitation, unless it should be England in the days of the Methodist revival in the first half of the eighteenth century.

With the latter movement, that of Hauge had very little, if anything, in common.

Neither Hauge nor his co-workers shouted, or caused any unseemly sensation, or appealed to the fear of hell, or said that one must necessarily be able to tell the day or hour of one's conversion, or roll on the ground, or go through violent contortions in order to prove the genuineness of the conversion. Perhaps for that reason (without in the least wishing to disparage other revivals) the Haugian movement was more sound and scriptural than those usually taking place in the Reformed churches. It will be of the utmost interest to mention, later on, some of the leading co-workers of Hauge, many of whom have well-known descendants both among ministers and laymen in this country. Here it will be timely to mention the names of some of the first missionaries. They were Hauge's two brothers, Ole Nielsen Hauge and Mikkel Nielsen Hauge; Paul Gundersen, the first man converted through Hauge, and his first cousin, Gundro V. Ramstad, also related to Hauge; Iver Olsen Gabestad from Troegstad, converted before he was of age, a born preacher, whom Hauge himself called a "chosen vessel" and gave the remarkable testimony that he was the foremost, most perfect Christian that had lived in Norway. One sentence of his was long remembered: "Some tell me that they are afraid of being converted, lest they do not remain Christian, and the last would then be worse than the first. I tell them that while it is true that there are those who begin who do not finish, it is also true that if they never begin, they will never finish."

76

Gabestad travelled as far north as Finmarken, but owing perhaps to the extremely early age at which he started to preach the Word, he later lost some of his fervor, but died in 1820 as a believing Christian in Drammen, where he had settled as a merchant.

Partly owing to the experience of Gabestad, the Haugian friends became extremely cautious in sending out very young men, and usually demanded that only men of ripe years and spiritual experience be permitted to go out as public speakers.

Then, again, there was Torkel Olsen Gabestad, a brother of the former, but a calmer and deeper nature. Elling Hansen Hoidal, also a cousin of Hauge, was a splendid type of a Haugian.

He travelled in Smaalenene and in the Bergen diocese, and settled in Romsdalen where he was highly respected as a lovable Christian character.

It would leave a wrong impression not to mention the one poor man who fell away. His name was Peder Hansen Roer. During the persecutions for Christ's sake he broke down spiritually, and to escape imprisonment denied the Lord who had bought him, a Demas among Hauge's followers, many of whom afterwards mentioned his name with tears in their eyes.

Soren Nielsen Roer was the first of them all to go outside of his own district, and in 1797 we find him in Numedal. He was a steady, active man, who became bailiff after Hauge's brother, and died in Rygge in 1853.

The importance of mentioning these names lies in the fact that it was often brought as an accusation against Hauge's friends, that they were men of "no account." Quite the contrary is the case. Almost without exception they were "men of substance," owners of property, business men and manufacturers;

and, as will be seen later, some of them became members of parliament.

Thus the Haugian movement had from the very start a broad, national basis.

If this little book was to give a history of Norway in the nineteenth century, it would show how the overthrow of the bureaucracy and the coming into its own of the Norwegian farmer element in politics and government as well as in national leadership generally, has its roots in the Haugian revival.

It was the very fear of a peasant uprising and a day of reckoning for the arrogant office holding class that made the latter, whether ecclesiastic or civil, desirous of crushing utterly Hauge and his revival. We must not be understood to mean that this was any part of Hauge's programme. Hauge was as loyal a man as ever lived. He always obeyed the law unless his conscience told him that he had to obey God first. He suffered Christian martyrdom. Any suggestion of insurrection would have struck him with horror. He never "resisted evil," but always turned the other cheek, though he remonstrated mildly against being treated illegally, and demanded justice at the hands of those who were bound by their oath of office to do justice.

But he had the rare manhood to refuse to beg for mercy when he knew he was innocent, and spurned an offer to escape from prison, when he understood that this offer was made in order to relieve a brutal government of the guilt of "judicial murder."

It is fortunately an established law in history that abuse of power reacts, sooner or later, against the violators of justice, and the broad lines of a democratic movement were unconsciously being drawn when Hauge and his friends set to work to preach the gospel in Norway.

As the Haugian movement progresses, we shall find that while it widens in scope and gains in definiteness, it also becomes gradually more and more complete, just as a living organism of healthy growth always seeks to develop every organ in order to possess the faculties needed for the attainment of its life-purpose.

Hauge had been called to be an evangelist, and he himself was step by step becoming conscious of possessing the full powers of an "ambassador of Christ." He could speak to individuals and to large gatherings, and he spoke with authority. He was afraid of no man, for God had spoken to him. He was called before ministers and magistrates, and he faced orderly courts and unruly mobs with the same imperturbable self-possession, the same Christian equanimity. He never seems even to have been excited. He set to work deliberately to formulate a programme for his work.

He unflinchingly challenged his adversaries. He was never taken by surprise. He was always ready to answer. No one ever silenced him.

One of the supreme needs of a movement like that of Hauge is literature. No great movement can live long without it.

Printing presses were already at work on several of his books. Perhaps no single individual in Norway kept presses more busy than he did. To begin with, he did not send out emissaries, but the movement was self-propagating. As far as the spiritual equipment was concerned, only one thing seemed wanting—that which is embodied in the admonition of the apostle Paul in his epistle to the Colossians, chapter 3, verse 16: "Let the word of Christ dwell in you richly in all wisdom; teaching and admonishing one another in psalms and hymns and spiritual songs, singing with grace in your hearts to the Lord." The Reformation created an entirely new hymnology, Luther himself being richly gifted as a writer of hymns. The Reformed revival of England produced a wonderful treasury of noble hymns. So did the pietistic movement. A lack of hymn writers is a sign of spiritual deadness. In fact, all great historical movements have been accompanied by an outburst of song. Of this, Dante in Italy, Shakespeare and Milton in England, Goethe and Schiller in Germany, Kingo and Brorson, and later Grundtvig and Oehlenschlaeger, in Denmark, as well as Wergeland, Bjørnson and Ibsen, Ivar Aasen and Osmund Olafson Vinje in Norway—to mention only a few of the better known—are illustrious examples. A great movement gains impetus and strength by having poetry and music attached to it. They act like wings. It is true that the Haugian movement did not produce great poetry. It had no use for that. But in the first place, Norway produced very little poetry in Hauge's day; and, in the second place, what the Haugian movement did produce was not only admirably fitted for its purpose, that of edification in small gatherings, but Hauge himself wrote the best Norweigan hymns produced till Landstad and Lindemann gave us the best hymn book Norway has had.

The first Haugian song-maker was, strangely enough, a young girl who died in Drammen in 1803, only twenty years old.

Her name is Larine Olsdaughter Oexne, from Lier, near Drammen. She was undoubtedly a highly gifted woman. Her heart was indeed a holy altar on which the fire of faith burned brightly. Her parents, who were well-to-do, considered it a disgrace that their daughter was become one of the "holy ones," and they refused her permission to attend the little assemblies of Hauge's friends.

Oh, the pity of such blindness!

In one song she describes her own conversion, the last two verses of which are as purely hymnological as anything found in our usual hymns, with the exception of the very best.

> "My Jesus, purify my soul,
>   And let me follow Thee alway,
> As well when I must drink the gall
>   As when I sing my joyful lay!
>
> Take thou my heart; whate'er betide,
>   Hold me with love's most tender cord,
> That I may be Thine own pure bride,
>   My God, my Savior, and my Lord!

This may certainly, with all due reverence, be called a "song of the bridal-chamber."

It is said that at one time, when a gathering was to be held in the neighborhood, her parents shut her up in the cellar. As she sat weeping in her lonliness, she felt so enraptured by the sense of the "Communion of Saints" that she composed the following Assembly Song, "just such a song," says Dr. Bishop Bang, "as is wont to be sung by true believers when they come together for the one purpose of serving the Lord. It shall have a place here," he continues, "in order to show how the fire from Hauge would flame up clear and pure where it was rightly received."

> "Jesus, Savior, in Thy name
>   We are gathered now to hear Thee.
> Let Thy Holy Spirit's flame
>   Sanctify us, bring us near Thee!
> Let Thy love our guardian be,
>   Thou our Lord, Thy children we.

By Thy grace the heavenly bread,
   E'er inviting, pleading ever,
On Thy table now is spread,
   We Thy guests, and Thou the Giver.
May Thy peace in heart and mind
   Us in sweet communion bind!

By Thy blood upon the Cross
   Thou from sin hast purified us.
All besides we count but loss,
   If Thou wilt but keep and guide us.
Jesus, for Thy sweat and pain,
   Let Thy word not sound in vain!

During the Christmas season of 1797, Hauge visited one of his relatives in Glemminge close to Fredriksstad. On the third day of Christmas he spoke to a small gathering on Tit. 2:11-15. The text is genuinely Haugian. While he was speaking, there entered the Rev. U. G. Feierman, accompanied by a lieutenant and three soldiers. Did they, perhaps, come to seek salvation? Oh, no. The minister had decided to crush the originator of the revival which had begun in his parish and which had both frightened and angered him. He demanded to know what Hauge was doing there. Hauge cited the text of his little sermon; but without further ado, the minister told Hauge to go with him, which he did immediately. He was taken to Fredriksstad where he was placed in the military prison. The intention was that the brutality of the soldiers should work on Hauge so that he should at once declare himself ready to desist from any further disturbance of the peace. What happens? Hauge spoke to the soldiers, and while some took his advice and were converted, others were enraged and threatened to put a gag in his mouth, bind him and flog him.

Hauge said they might do with him as they pleased; but for his part, he had never heard of any one being thus maltreated.

One of the soldiers who was in jail with Hauge sang an indecent song:

"I presume," said Hauge mildly, "that your mother taught you that song?"

"Shut your mouth. Don't mention her to me."

"Perhaps she is dead?"

The face of the soldier trembled with emotion.

"That's none of your business."

"No, no; but I just happened to think that if she were alive, she would perhaps not feel so overly happy just now."

There was a moment's silence.

"Isn't it all the same to you what she is?"

Hauge looked down.

"Such a voice as you have," he said tenderly, "could be used for something better."

"Why are you here, then?"

"I sang just as you do, and so they put me here. I read the Word of God and sang."

"Then you are one of these 'holy fellows'?"

"Bosh," exclaimed another, mockingly.

Hauge answered slowly, without looking at any one in particular:

"When one tries to turn folks away from that which is evil, so that their mothers need not weep over them, they send one in here. I suppose that is why you are here also?"

Then the jailer came to announce dinner for the prison guests.

As Hauge rose to go, he turned to the one who had been singing and said, as he put his hand kindly on his shoulder:

"Don't be angry with me for what I said; but I felt so sure that you might become a child of God."

The young soldier weakened. The coarseness of his face changed and became more soft. His eyes were warm.

83

"I don't think so," he said. Then he turned away and wept.

Hauge waited a while.

"Yes," he said softly, "I am quite sure of it now."

The soldier tried to stop his tears, turned to Hauge and said: "My mother died last spring."

"But God is not dead," answered Hauge. "If you keep yourself to Him, perhaps we shall meet again."

"Then you must help me."

"Certainly I shall," answered Hauge.

The jailer came just then: "What is going on here?" he said brusquely.

"Only that which is good," Hauge said, and looked at the jailer with one of his soul-winning smiles.

To stop Hauge from speaking to the prisoners and singing, they now put him in the "Iron Cage," a solitary cell, with no fire and an open window. The reader must remember that this was at Christmas in Norway, in the year 1797.

"Birds like you," said the watchman, "must be in a cage. Now you can sing all you want." We shall let Jacob B. Bull tell the wonderful story: "And Hauge did sing, so that many of the soldiers were moved to tears. All through the still, cold winter night hymns floated out in the darkness, a rich, lonely voice, tender and strong.

Hans Nielsen Hauge, the farmer boy from Tune, sang in his cage—a prayer for light in the darkness!

In his cage Hauge remained all of next day. Towards evening, as he experienced a peculiar cool weariness, he fell on his knees on the cold floor, folded his hands and prayed.

Beautiful visions arose in his soul. He felt as if God was close to him. Was he soaring away into the sky, was his soul freed from its earthly encumbrance? All was white. The frost and the snow-white fields looked as if a white peace had covered the earth as he fled from it. He seemed to sense the flutter of white wings about him. He was carried towards ever growing light high up.

"Ah," he said as if in a trance to himself, "death is exceedingly white and beautiful as light. Soon I shall see the face of my God." And he shut his eyes to die.

Suddenly he awoke. A man in a corporal's unifrom stood over him.

"You are freezing," he said, as Hauge rose to his feet and sat down.

"Yes," he said languidly, "I believe I am cold." The corporal looked about him.

"This is indefensible," he said. "It is barbarous to let a man sit in here in mid-winter."

Hauge looked up in astonishment. Did any one really have pity?

"God bless you," he said.

The corporal looked at him. Then he went to the little table and took the lantern he had brought.

"This won't do," he said with some feeling, "this is utterly inhuman."

"Well," Hauge said, "men become worse than devils when they are godless."

The corporal did not answer. He opened the heavy door and said: "Come now. You are not to remain here tonight. Tomorrow you will be brought to the bailiff, Mr. Radich, for trial."

The face of Hauge colored slightly.

"You come as if the Lord had sent you."

The corporal smiled. Then a voice outside called out: "Corporal Blegen!"

"Yes, lieutenant."

"Be quick there!"

"Yes, lieutenant."

85

Then the lieutenant led the procession with his sword drawn, and, followed by the corporal, Hauge was lodged in his former cell.

Next morning a seat-cart was ready, and in it sat Hauge guarded by the corporal.

"Watch the prisoner, Blegen," said the lieutenant.

"Yes, sir," said the corporal.

Then the seat-cart drove off to the bailiff's.

It was a long trial, but resulted in nothing. Next day Hauge was again taken back to Fredriksstad.

"You are a strange man," said the corporal, "you could be free tomorrow if you but promised not to hold those meetings. And then you prefer to be in prison!"

Hauge smiled.

"The day is coming when you will do just as I am doing. But first of all you must learn to know God."

They drove on in silence; but the corporal could not get out of his mind this strange strong, quiet man who would rather be in prison and have peace with God, than to be at liberty and have peace with the world. When they alighted, Hauge took the hand of the corporal.

"I thank you for your kindness," he said. "Some day we shall meet where there is real happiness."

"I thank you," said the corporal.

* * *

And who was this Corporal Blegen? And what happened to him? Before long he was a converted man. His superiors became enraged. A soldier to be one of Hauge's adherents, praying, reading the Bible! Scandalous!

One day, an officer stood before him with drawn sword and compelled him with terrible oaths to take an emetic.

"Yes, but I am not sick," said the Corporal.

86

"Never mind," said the officer, "I want you to take it so you can throw up the Holy Ghost."

This made no difference to Corporal Blegen, who had seen that Hauge suffered without complaining.

He got his discharge, as he might spread the poison further in the army. Returning to his farm in the Faaberg parish, near Lillehammer, his home soon became the center of Christian influence during half a century. He was a man of intellect, deeply religious, yet of a lively disposition, very industrious, and one of the most highly respected men in his district. His name was Johan Torgerson Blegen.

*  *  *

Many and peculiar were the incidents that occurred in connection with Hauge's arrest in Fredriksstad. Great crowds gathered to get a look at this strange man from Tune. Some pitied him, while others treated him with contumely. His friends were in deep sorrow.

When the news came to his home, his mother was nearly frantic.

"What will they do with him?" she cried.

"Do not be alarmed," the father said. "Hans will pull through all right."

And Hans did.

Hauge left the jail in Fredriksstad on the 29th of January, 1798. The sheriff ordered Hauge set at liberty, saying that the minister, the Reverend Mr. Feierman, had exceeded his authority in reading only the 14th and 15th paragraphs of the Conventicle Act, without carefully noting what was said in the 8th, the 12th and the 17th.

When Hauge was told that he was released from prison, he said that according to Acts 16, 37, the parish minister ought to come and bring him out of the prison in person.

But Feierman was not that kind of a "man."

So Hauge was free to go home.

Feierman was nearly beside himself with rage.

He could never afterwards see one of Hauge's friends without flying off the handle.

One Sunday forenoon two of them wished to partake of the Lord's Supper in Feierman's church. In those days, the communicants had to appear individually before the minister to be admitted to the Lord's Table. The minister no sooner understood who those two men were, than he took a long whip, struck at the two men fiercely and with all his might, and chased them out of the church. That was all the "communion" those men got that Sunday.

Meantime, as usually happens, the most ridiculous rumors circulated about Hauge.

Some said that he worshipped "wooden images," that he pretended to perform miracles, that he practiced the most degrading vices, that he was an adulterer, a thief, and a drunkard. His trial helped to set some of these rumors at rest, but many of them were widely circulated and followed Hauge from place to place. He was the most talked-about man in Norway.

The trial in Fredriksstad had established two facts: Hauge was not to be silenced till he had his work done, and the sheriff of Smaalene, Mr. Hofgaard, had still further reprimanded the fiery Mr. Feierman by letting him and the officious Mr. Radich know that as far as he had been able to ascertain, the friends of Hauge, whom they were persecuting, were very respectable, industrious and moral people, while Hauge himself was spoken of by all as a man highly respected by the common people, who heard him gladly. They understood him and were edified by him. He had heard people say that Hauge, far from encouraging idleness, was himself a very industrious man, that his preaching cost them nothing, that they neither ate nor drank at their gatherings, and that they thought it much better to go to such meetings as those of Hauge than to visit drink shops and dance halls where much that was against the law was being practiced without any interference on the part of the authorities. "I advise you not to persecute Hauge," wrote Sheriff Hofgaard, "he might easily, highly gifted and respected as he is, become an agitator and start something or other."

Here was at least one man who would have agreed with Gamaliel of Jerusalem—a very rare instance at that time.

Most people would suppose that Hauge had had enough in Fredriksstad and would remain quiet for a while. "The love of Christ is constraining me," would have been Hauge's answer to any suggestion that he give up.

Besides, he had to let his friends know what was going on. Not a week had gone by since Hauge's return home when he had ready his next book, in which he gives a brief account of his experiences in Fredriksstad and adds an exposition of the epistle lesson and the gospel for All Saint's Day.

Hauge's authorship is absolutely logical. Every book he had written so far and all he wrote afterwards was simply another way of doing what the Lord had called him to do. It all grew spontaneously as it were, out of his very life-soil. His books are so many heart-throbs of a man so eager to serve the Lord that he could not let a moment slip by. Of Hauge it is no exaggeration to use the words of the Psalmist: "Zeal of Thine house hath eaten me up." Ps. 69:9.

With the manuscript in his pocket Hauge set out once more for Christiania, thence through Romerike

89

to the Grundset Fair, and then from Elverum back to Tune.

Later in the spring he again visited Christiania, where he had now won many friends, among them Anders Kristoffersen Groendahl, father of the later well-known printer, Chr. A. Groendahl, who also was converted and became a lay-preacher. The younger Groendahl went to Copenhagen with Hauge, learned the book-printing business, became foreman in the printing business of H. T. Bakkerud in Christianssand, and in 1812, assisted by Count Wedel-Jarlsberg, established a printing business of his own and is known as the first man in Norway who used a speed printing press. During his stay in Christiania, Hauge was twice arrested and sent home.

No sooner had Hauge arrived home than he set out on a longer journey. About midsummer he took ship in Drammen for Bergen. The ship was "calmed" before it reached Bergen, and Hauge was taken in a row boat to the city, a distance of close to eighty miles.

Johan Nordahl Brun was then assistant bishop of the diocese, as the bishop, Dr. Ole Irgens, was very old and entirely blind. In no city was Hauge so well treated as here, where the mighty personality of Bishop Brun protected him. When persecution was about to start, Brun rose in his power and told the ministers that "it was their duty to preach just what Hauge was preaching.

"Hauge might not be a high class preacher, but he had himself heard ministers who served out worse nonsense than Hauge did. Anyway, Hauge's work was harmless, and as long as he (Brun) had anything to say, no one should do him any harm." While Bishop Brun, Norway's greatest orator at that time, did not understand the real significance of the Haugian

90

movement, his hatred of injustice caused him to hold his protecting shield over him—the only high churchman in Norway who dared to do this.

In his answer to the authorities, Brun makes the very pertinent remark, that "if the Conventicle Act is legally (de jure) in force, it is a very antiquated piece of legislation which is actually (de facto) out of date and should be disregarded; for what sense is there in forbidding an unlearned man to preach the gospel to a handful of people, when 'half-learned' men are writing against the Word of God for millions?"

In Bergen, Hauge met a sect of people who in their meetings went into a trance, spoke with tongues, did not wear shoes without laces, and did not eat anything that had the blood of any animal in it, while the men were not permitted to shave. Hauge convinced them with the words of Christ that it is not what enters into the mouth that makes man unclean.

He also found here adherents of the famous German mystic Jacob Boehme. It is strange how in every place Hauge got in touch with people whom no one else seemed able to reach—and by his staunch scriptural evangelism wins them back to the good old paths. He is, in fact, a true missionary of a very superior kind.

Two extremes met in Bergen at this time, which, it should be noted, is the time of the French Revolution and the beginning of the Napoleonic era.

In no city of Norway was true Christianity so forcefully and faithfully preached, while at the same time there was a good deal of freethinking and political radicalism found among the upper classes, as was also the case in Christiania, where the French Revolution was given "all hail" and "welcome" by some of the foremost and richest men of the capital. These Hauge, of course, could not reach. But Johan Nordal

91

Brun thundered against them and their "Jacobine club," and held them in awe. Besides Brun, there was the kindly, pious, and humble minister at the Church of the Cross, Johan Sebastian Cammermeyer, grandfather of the poet Welhaven, who bore his name, the cathedral minister Knut Gelmuyden Fleischer, and the curate Marcus Fred'k Irgens, the old bishop's son. Thus Bergen became to Hauge a veritable Bethany, where he was well treated, and never seriously molested.

Hauge found his best friends among those who had been awakened by the famous bishop Erich Pontoppidan, whose theology (if Hauge may be said to have systematized his teaching to such an extent that it can be dignified with such an august title) he had adopted "in toto." Hauge was an out and out "Pontoppidaner" —all honor to him for it!

For this he was rewarded by the very valuable friendship of one who had been the bishop's housekeeper, Miss Maren Boes. She was now about seventy years old, a lovely Christian woman, whose interview with Hauge (real or imagined) should be read in Bull's excellent story of Hauge. The one paragraph in which Hauge's interview with Maren Boes is described is worth more than dollars and cents.

"I want to thank you," she said, as he clasped her old, rheumatic hand. "You have edified me. Yes, that is God's white truth. You have made me, an old woman, young again. To hear you was just like hearing my old saintly master, the Right Reverend Erich Pontoppidan himself. You sent us a breath of the Holy Spirit, you see. That was real 'must and marrow.' It was the 'seed corn of God.' Thanks, and God's blessing for today. But you must come to my apartment and see me. I want more of the same kind."

92

Maren Boes was well-to-do and she was disappointed when Hauge later refused her offer of all her money to start business in Bergen and settle there. The story may as well be told here, though it did not happen till Hauge visited Bergen a second time. She asked him to come and see her, and waited for him, dressed in all her finery.

"You must sit down, Hauge," she said. "I have something to talk to you about."

Hauge seated himself.

"Well," she said, as she took her staff in her trembling hands, "you are suffering so much for our Lord's cause that my heart has gone out to you in great tenderness on account of all your persecutions and tribulations." She moved her staff and rocked her little body as she continued: "It is just like this: I am quite well-to-do; I have much property, and I'll soon be going home. So I thought I would like to leave it all to you—if you would come to Bergen and settle down."

She looked warmly at Hauge.

"Now, what do you say to that?"

Hauge's face grew pale, and tears came into his eyes, as he answered calmly: "I am indeed grateful to you for the kindness you wish to show me, but I could not accept the offer, if you gave me the whole city of Bergen."

Maren Boes moved backward as if she had received a blow.

"What do you say!" she exclaimed.

"No, not if you offered me the whole city of Bergen," Hauge repeated. His voice was firm as he spoke.

"And why not," she asked.

"Just for the Lord's sake. It would indeed be a great pleasure for me to stay here among so many dear friends. But think of all those all over this land who are waiting to hear a Word of God! I would commit mortal sin if I did this. I should be in hell-fire all the time."

Maren Boes sat silent for just a moment. Then she arose and approached Hauge.

"Now I want to hold your hand." She seized it and held it firmly in both of her own.

"You are a man of sterling worth, Hauge. God bless you. And fare you now where you wish and must. I am not going to tempt you any more, much as I should like to see you here."

While in Bergen on his first visit, Hauge published two more books. The first one he had written at home after his return from Christiania, and it bears the earmarks of his experiences from his two arrests and his later meeting with a schoolmaster who acted like a madman towards him, used profane language, struck him, drove him out of a house which was not his own, and would barely permit him to put on his overcoat, though it was bitter cold.

"It is a good thing to have warm clothes, when it is cold," Hauge had said as he left, "and still better to be armed with the love of Christ, so that I can pray for those which despitefully use me and perse-cute me. May the peace of God be with you. Fare-well." Hauge walked quietly away.

Then something happened.

The schoolmaster ran out on the stoop and stood looking wonderingly at this strange man. Then all of a sudden he burst into tears. "Merciful God," he exclaimed, "what have I done?" Then he wept vio-lently.

A moment later he started on a run after Hauge. "Stay," he shouted into the darkness, "where are you?"

"Here," said Hauge calmly.

"Can you forgive me?" the teacher sobbed.

"Certainly," answered Hauge. "God forgives every one."

Hauge started to walk away.

"No, no, don't go," the teacher cried.

"Yes," said a voice away in the darkness, "it must so be."

The teacher stood on the stoop, wringing his hands. "Where are you going?"

"Where God leads me."

"Fare thee well, then, and may you have a good journey."

"Welcome after yourself." The words came softly from the distance.

"And it was night." Such a man!

Out of these experiences Hauge wrote his book: "The Teaching for the Simple-minded and the Strength of the Weak."

Of this book Dr. Bang says that "it lightens and thunders and sparkles to all sides, as if he had been hammering a piece of red hot iron."

The other book, published in Bergen at the same time, contained a number of remarkable passages from the Bible, especially such as refer to conversion, faith and sanctification. How shall one explain that Prof. Steenersen, of the University of Christiania, called this "a strange book"?

One other man, whom Hauge met in Bergen, and who became one of his most devoted friends, was Samson Thorbjoernsen Traae, born in Hardanger, who was a soldier of the garrison in Bergen for ten years, from 1789 to 1799. It was he who together with Ole Roersveen stood outside the prison in Christiania that Christmas Eve when Hauge put the candle in the window. To be a friend of Hauge at that time was a mark of nobility.

---

Hauge left Bergen in the beginning of November, again taking ship. This time contrary winds hindered his progress, and in order not to waste any time, he hired an open boat and rowed the rest of the way to Stavanger.

Could nothing stop that man?

Wherever Hauge travelled, he paid close attention to the character, customs, dress, manners, and way of living of the people he met. Naturally, his observations always have a strictly ethical ring.

This he did—the words are his own—in order to know better how to win their hearts for God and His Word. In his own neighborhood, Smaalenene, and around Christiania, foreign styles had made inroads on the national dress. In certain districts, the men kept their national costumes longer than the women. He tells us, with something of pardonable pride in his words, that there was a little more culture among the people of his own immediate neighborhood. He calls it "the circle in which I was born." People there were quite social and benevolent, although some were covetous and ignorant, while others were given to finery of dress and sensuality. In the counties of Akershus and Buskerud he found less willingness among the people to hear his message. In Smaalenene it was quite common for a father to gather his folks for family worship.

In the cities he found a great deal of frivolity, vanity, and freethinking.

We shall see later on how true this was as to the so-called "Upper Tendom" in Christiania.

It was perhaps in Bergen that Hauge became better informed as to the chief source of the freethinking then quite prevalent among the upper classes, since he says that "Voltaire and his successors with their licentious, freethinking, and irreligious conceits had taught people to ridicule the Bible and religion in general," and he ascribes this as the cause of the awful happenings in France, as well as in other countries, even in Norway.

About the people in Bergen, he speaks in terms of admiration, noting particularly that the men of the city were "plainly dressed," which he says he likes best.

There seems to underlie this a concession to the women, a fine touch of esthetic appreciation of the beautiful. While he would naturally condemn dandyism as utterly unmanly, he no doubt could allow something for the feminine weakness of wishing to look well. And who would not like him the more for it? But he is very plain-spoken about the "Striler " (the people of Hordaland), some of whom, he says, seemed to live more like animals than human beings. He visited places where it was all he could do to sit down and eat. "I found among them," he says, "very little desire to cultivate either their land, heart, or mind, too much clinging to the customs of their ancestors, though," he adds—what clear ideas did not Hauge have—"it may be excused, since it helps to preserve the old Norwegian simplicity and frugality."

Between Stavanger and Christianssand he found but few that cared for spiritual matters. They seemed too much absorbed in wickedness, profit, and sensual pleasures, unwilling to do anything for others, very selfish, which latter characteristic he applies particularly to the people living east of Christianssand, between Arendal and Skien.

But there was one exception—Lister. And this exception is so rare and so strongly marked, that it will occupy us for a little while, especially as it will bring to our attention "the most enigmatic character in Norway at that time." Perhaps it would be hard to find his parallel at any time.

From Stavanger he walked along the coast of Jaederen, everywhere distributing his writings and preaching conversion.

Then he came to Lister. With the parish of Vanse as a center, this was a spiritual oasis in Norway at that time. The former dean, Soeren Bugge, had been a warmhearted Christian who leaned strongly towards the Moravians (Herrnhutians). Bishop Bang characterizes him as one of the finest pastoral types of that day. He was the parish minister in Vanse from 1767 to 1790, and Bishop Pavels declares that half of Lister was "Herrnhutian." In 1790 the old dean, "without his knowledge and against his will" was transferred to the rich and much easier parish of Oeiestad, in the eastern part of the country, where he died in 1794. His son, the famous Mag. Peter Olivarius Bugge, became his successor. So eager were the people of Vanse to get the younger Bugge as their minister that they sent a committee to Copenhagen to request his appointment.

The purpose of giving space to the description of one or two ministerial characters among the Norwegian clergymen of Hauge's time, is to show what Hauge had to contend with in his attempt to evangelize Norway.

Dr. Bang thus describes this most "enigmatic" personality in the history of the Norwegian Church. There was, he says, a sad duplicity in him. He was now one thing, then again the very opposite. At times a strict Herrnhutian, then again the most outspoken rationalist. One day he would hold a devotional meeting in his parsonage and be one of a small

98

gathering of devoted Christians. The next day he would have a card-party with the most worldly people from Farsund and lose at cards his whole offering. On occasions he would defend the simple - minded Christians of his parish, and then again he would call them "foolish beasts" and "big scamps."

Peter Olivarius Bugge was born December 2, 1764, and died as retired bishop of Trondhjem in 1849.

During his childhood he was under the severest Christian discipline in his home. Later he spent some years with his uncle Hans Wilhelm Bugge in Bergen. This uncle travelled a great deal, visited Herrnhut in 1751, where he met Renatus Zinzendorph, and after a few years' stay in Copenhagen returned to Herrnhut, where he met Count Zinzendorph himself. In 1770 he was sent to Bergen to look after the Moravian Brethren there, and left Bergen in 1784.

In 1776 his nephew Peter Olivarius came to Bergen, just as the uncle was called to Herrnhut for a short visit, and he took the young Peter Olivarius along. This was in the spring, and they returned to Bergen in September.

In Herrnhut the young man had to read out of the Greek New Testament to Spangenberg, the other leader of the Moravian Brethren, before he would give him his blessing. The impression left on the young man must have been very strong, but his temperament, which was extraordinarily lively, may at times have rebelled against the restraints imposed upon him. He remained in Bergen four years, till 1780. Later he studied in Christianssand, and was prepared for his graduation, together with his friend Chr. Soerensen, by the famous Latin scholar Soeren Monrad, who later became bishop of Christianssand. He took his theological examination in 1786, and had at the age of 22 been appointed a curate in his father's parish, when his professor in Copenhagen, Moldenhauer, informed him in a letter from Spain that he had appointed him to a charge in Denmark, to which the university had "alternate advowson." The three years he spent in Denmark were not happy years, perhaps on account of the distance at which he was kept by the proprietor of Skullelev manor, Count von Scheel Plessen. He was permitted to put up his horse in the Count's stable, but he himself had to be satisfied with the servants' hall for a dressing-room. This treatment would be a constant cause of irritation to a Norwegian of Bugge's type. He did not like Denmark and the Danes, and in 1790 he requested to be transferred to Vanse as his father's successor.

While he still preached Herrnhutian sermons, and held devotional meetings in his parsonage, it did not take long before he was considered an "apostate." A well-known man in Vanse at that time, O. K. Vatne, says that he very soon showed that it was not his intention to become what his father had been: an out and out Herrnhutian.

Another witness, F. T. Knudsen, tells that he became "thoroughly worldly."

Yet when he sought the charge after the famous and learned Prof. Dr. Hans Strom in Eker, twenty-four farmers in Vanse sent a special request to the king, asking that Bugge remain in Vanse, saying in the petition that "we are some thousands of people in number who are ready to declare that we never can get a man who can do so much for us as our present teacher." Perhaps this expression of devotedness made the young and highly gifted minister feel that after this he need not be so careful in his way of living. That he did not satisfy the strictest of the Hernhutians in Vanse is proven by the petition which two of them in 1793 sent to the Danish government office, asking that they be permitted to hold "godly conventicles" on the following conditions: 1. That they attend the ordinary church services and receive the sacrament from the officiating minister. 2. That they undertake nothing contrary to the Word of God and the Royal Ordinances, and that their meetings be open to the parish minister whenever he may wish to be present. 3. That six of their own men be chosen by themselves with power to accept or reject members, and that none others than persons thus admitted attend their gatherings, and also that none be permitted to disturb the peace. 4. That they be permitted to build, if they feel able, a large room where their meetings may be held, and 5. That they be permitted to call a man who is fit and acceptable to them from the Moravian Society, that he may edify them whenever their own pastors are prevented from doing so.

This is, no doubt, the first attempt in Norway to organize a congregation along lines with which we in this country are quite familiar. And it is the first step towards the building of the meeting houses which later became common enough in that part of the country. They were called "houses of prayer" (Bethels).

The petition was, of course, denied, especially on account of the three last points. The things mentioned in the first two were already permissible by the "Conventicle Act" of 1741.

Hauge remained in Vanse a while, and is said to have visited the famous Mag. P. O. Bugge, the parish minister.

A tradition, the historicity of which is vouched for by Dr. Bang and Jacob B. Bull, but is questioned by Daniel Thrap, says that when Hauge visited Bugge, the latter told him that "even if a multitude of ministers rise up against you, yes, even if I should oppose you, keep right on, for the future belongs to you."

Whether he said it or not, it would have been the truth if he had said it. To Hauge, Bugge's attitude would have made no difference.

Bugge left Vanse in 1799 and did not see Hauge again till 1815 or 1816, in Christiania.

As bishop of Trondhjem he declared publicly in 1804, the same year in which he became bishop and Hauge was imprisoned in Christiania: "Also I believe that Hauge is a rogue and ought to be treated as a rouge. I have never seen Hauge or any of his adherents." (The word rogue in this connection is supposed to refer not to Hauge's religious work, but to his business transactions.)

As a member of parliament in 1816, Bugge expressed a desire to see Hauge, who was then again a free man, and highly respected so that many of the leading men came to see him. Prof. Hersleb got his cousin, the Rev. P. C. H. Kjerschow, to invite Hauge and at his house Bugge together with his son, Soeren B. Bugge, then student, Prof. Hersleb, and his nephew J. O. H. Walnum, then only 17 years old, met and talked with Hauge; but when Hauge noticed that Bugge tried to pump him, he became silent. Such a "mise en scene" for curiosity's sake was not to Hauge's taste. Spiritually and morally, Hauge was a bigger man than Bugge.

It will be interesting to look into the literary productions of this "most highly gifted" man, whose duplicity is as sharply drawn in his books as in his character.

In 1790, when he came to Vanse as pastor, he had already written a book of sermons. It is said that he made up his mind to write one sermon each evening, which he did. The sermons were published in 1791, in Copenhagen, and became very popular, being translated into Swedish, German, Dutch, and Finnish.

These sermons are so orthodox and so full of Hern-hutian Christianity, that he has been accused of publishing his father's sermons. In the preface to the second edition he says that he does not want to be classed with those who teach that "one has only to believe in the redemption of Christ, otherwise live at pleasure." This was the rationalistic idea of Herrn-hutism.

In 1795 he wrote a doctor's thesis, which he sent to the university of Goettingen in Germany. The title of it is: "About the moral depravity of man, its origin and general character." For this he was created a doctor of theology. Now, how does the author of a "Moravian" book of sermons treat this tremendously important subject?

Evidently, to be a minister for the good people of Vanse, Lister, in Norway, was something entirely different from being a "doctor of theology" in Goettin-gen. In his doctor's thesis he says: "Some theolo-gains say that man's depravity is so great that he has in him the tendency to every vice, while he is incapable of any good; but every one must understand that this is contrary to all reason." Again: "Unfortunately, Augustin introduced the idea of "original sin"; Hugh of St. Victor brought it out again, and it finally got into the Augusburg Confession. . . . This doctrine has been the cause of the most terrible errors."

In his thesis, Bugge does not want to know anything about a devil, and does not blame him for man's fall in sin. "With the aid of religion," he says, "man is capable of regaining the lost image of God, i.e., virtue may become his nature, and temptation to sin will gradually lose its power."

Bugge's double attitude reminds us of a professor of theology who delivered a sermon to a group of ministers, without offering any prayer. When asked why he omitted the prayer, he answered, as a learned professor should, that the sermon was not an ordinary sermon, but an "academic" one. Verily, learning is a great thing!

In 1799 he left Vanse and was minister in Fredericia, Denmark, till 1804, when he became bishop.

Nobody will deny that Bugge as bishop was an energetic administrator and a man who did not spare himself. Nor did he spare others. He hit right and left, high and low, and was considered a type of an independent Norwegian. The good people of Trondhjem thought different after Bugge's coronation sermon, when Carl Johan was crowned. His windows were stoned. The Constitution, Bugge described as "miserable."

He was always in trouble with the Danish Government office. It was a period of utter decadence. Chaos seemed to reign everywhere. The church of Norway actually declared itself unable to cope with the difficulties of the times, which were great indeed. It went practically into spiritual, and almost into economic, bankruptcy. It was unable to meet the storm. The only one who met it manfully and effectively was Hauge. And Hauge was finally imprisoned for good in the very year in which Bugge became bishop of Trondhjem, just when he could have been of the greatest service. A brief account of conditions will prove this.

Bugge found in his diocese a number of good men; but a large number of them were such that it is a pity one has to tell about them. Without doing so, however, one would not quite understand the blessing and necessity of Hauge's work.

The story of Jacob Krogh Borch is not typical, but exceedingly illustrative.

Born in Christiania in 1770, just one year before

Hauge, he took all his degrees with distinction. In Copenhagen he wasted his father's money in riotous living, so he was called home and told to shift for himself. Tired of living in small circumstances he again went to Copenhagen, where, at a court ball, he stole the bejeweled hat of the royal heir-presumptive Frederick.

Then he became an actor in Stockholm and Gothenburg, but found his associates so morally depraved that he returned home. The father, who was a wealthy merchant at the "Vaterland Bridge" in Christiania, established him in the liquor business, which he found (to his credit be it said) abominable. When the "Dramatic Society" was started in Christiania, Borch became one of its best actors. Then, when his father died in 1802, he collected all the funds he could get hold of, went to Copenhagen, and in two years (1802-1804) prepared himself for and took his theological examination. This was April 30th. Already May 3rd he was appointed curate in Oerkedalen, in the Trondhjem diocese. He was ordained September 13, 1805, delivered his ordination sermon, and was installed in his charge on the 17th Sunday after Trinity, at the same time assisting with the "Communion."

Here again he delivered the same sermon, but made a mess of it, and could not say the Lord's Prayer. This in spite of his cleverness as an actor.

The following Sunday he preached in the annex church of Skogn. Here also there was to be Communion. When the confessional hymn had been sung, Borch turned to the parish-clerk and said: "What shall I do next?"

Parish-clerk: "Take the people by the hand."

Borch: "What next?"

Parish-clerk: "Deliver the Communion sermon."

Then he read a few words from a piece of paper and said: "Now what next?"

Parish-clerk: "Absolve the cummunicants?"

This was something entirely new, so the clerk had to ask him to put his hands on the heads of the communicants while the clerk pronounced the words of absolution. And thus all the way through, till the congregation started to laugh aloud.

Then he delivered his ordination sermon a third time, but stumbled at the Lord's Prayer, although he had written it down. When he was through, he beckoned to the clerk, who continued to sing, while the congregation was in a terrible uproar.

He knew that he had to read his "Letter of presentation and collation" (bishop's certificate); but when he had read Trondhjem, September 13, 1805, Bugge," he left the pulpit without another word.

There was to be a baptism at the same service, but when the time came that he was to place his hand on the child's head, he placed it on the head of the woman who held the child. At the earnest appeal of the parish-clerk, he was permitted to finish the Communion service. But a few days after, a committee came to the parish minister, Dean Coldevin, and told him that if Borch ever came back, they would all leave the church and refuse to use him for any churchly doings. The dean pacified them, and they promised to hear him once more before they reported him to the bishop, Peter Olivarius Bugge.

On the 19th Sunday after Trinity Borch delivered his ordination sermon the fourth time. Finally, he was prevailed upon to resign on a pension. He had then been a minister less than two months. The pension was given him because he had been found "entirely incapable" as a minister. He had evidently considered the ministry like any other trade, one moreover that one could enter when everything else had been a failure.

In the parish of Bjoernoer, it was quite common to see the communicants staggering up to the altar in the most extreme condition of intoxication.

In the above mentioned Skogn parish there was a minister, a Dane, Christian von Haven by name. When the farmers sent in their complaint to the bishop saying that they could not use him, the bishop wrote to v. Haven that if he did not wish to be deposed, he must be sober at least one day each week.

While even men like Bishop Brun declared that Hauge and his associates preached "pious nonsense," it was Bishop Bugge who said about the theological candidates from Copenhagen that they learned nothing of what they really had use for in their ministry.

The complaint was general that the ministry had sunk so low in the general estimation that men of parts entered into more lucrative occupations. Some there were who felt that something must be done to improve matters, or the Church would soon lose all its influence.

The relation between the parish minister and the curate in the cities was unsatisfactory, as people looked upon the poor curate as an inferior being.

It was then proposed that both ministers should be called co-pastors (they have that appellation in Sweden), and exchange services, while the income should be divided equally between them, but the minister who had served the lonnger time should have the best farm. No attention was paid to this proposal.

Another proposal was due to the great lack of ministers, many parishes being without a pastor for many years. In 1827 the following parishes were without a pastor in the diocese of Trondhjem alone: Bjoernoer,

Opdal, Gryten, Boe, Edoe, Naero, Christianssund, Kvernes, and Grip.

In this emergency, Niels Treschow proposed to make use of non-theological ministers, i.e., lay-preachers. Had he been able to propose such a thing but for the work of Hauge? It is done in Norway today. But when the proposition was sent to Bishop Bugge, in 1818, he could with difficulty suppress the feeling of disgust that overcame him at the very thought of it. His opinion was that the cure would be worse than the disease. If men could become ministers without studying theology, few would care to study at all.

If such a misfortune should occur, he would prefer to let the non-theological ministers administer the sacraments (a rather novel idea, to be sure) while the department would have it the other way around. He proposed that a book of sermons be published on texts from both testaments, from which such a man could read a sermon at services where no ordained man was present, while a supply pastor could visit these churches at least five or six times a year. The other man should not be ordained and should not be called a minister, but a "superintendent," and should perform such work as to prepare the Confirmation class, catechise, bid the banns and conduct funerals. Bugge seemed to see the Church swamped by unfortunate lawyers, office clerks, non-commissioned officers and others, and he concludes by saying: "May God in His mercy save the Church!"

Yet, it was this very thing, which Bishop Bugge loathed to think about, i.e., the Haugian lay-preaching, which saved the Church, until such a time as the new crop of theologically educated men with gospel training should have prepared themselves in sufficient numbers for service in the churches of Norway.

This work did not begin till 1813. Three men became theological candidates in 1815, two in 1816, one in 1817. In 1818 there were thirteen. The condition of the church buildings was sometimes beyond description. In some, the altar ring had been removed—rotted down. In others the vestments were so filthy that a minister asked if it were necessary for him to use them. In still another there was a baptistry built in addition to the church, which was so cold that the women with their children were exposed to great hardships during the long service.

Confession was so arranged that the upper class came Thursday while the working people came Saturday. Complaint of this was sent to the bishop, with the question, if all were not equal before God? The answer of the bishop is characteristic. He said: "Just because all are equal, each one should have the privilege of 'undisturbed worship,' and that was not possible where a refined lady had to kneel down alongside of a sailor who smelt strongly of pitch and tobacco. It was, moreover, the opinion of the bishop that the minister could do more good if he divided those who came to confession into classes, as newlyweds by themselves, those newly confirmed by themselves, soldiers by themselves, and so forth. Whether he meant that blacksmiths, tailors, lawyers, and other professional men should come, each trade or profession by itself, does not appear from the records.

Some ministers asked if they might not in cases of necessity use self-communion. He thought there was nothing reprehensible in this, but sent the question "higher up." During the war, wine became scarce, and one minister after another wanted to know whether red wine could be used instead of the white wine which was no longer to be had. This was easily answered. But when even the red wine could not

109

be had, one minister wanted to know if it was absolutely necessary to use wine, and the bishop answered that he would be deposed from his office if he used anything else. From Lund, Oerlandet, came the report that the congregation was willing to use water instead of wine. The bishop had no words with which to express his opinion of a congregation so utterly ignorant.

Dean Stub proposed to limit communion to one annually, as otherwise the owners of churches would be ruined. In one case it was found that a certain farmer had had his child baptised at home in "beer."

Grain was as scarce as wine, and in 1813 Bishop Bugge feared that half of the congregation in his diocese would starve to death. When Hauge during the incumbency of Bugge's predecessor, Schoenheyder, came to Trondhjem with a load of seed corn, he told him that he was welcome with his seed for free distribution, but he must not preach the Word of God.

During these hard times, a farmer had cut down two pine trees belonging to a captain in the army, in order to get the bark to save his family from starvation. This fine captain, whose name we fortunately do not know, haled the poor man before the Board of Conciliation and compelled him to pay a fine of one thousand dollars for the offense.

When the bishop in 1817 had three churches which he should dedicate, in Hevne, Vaerdalen, and Stoeren, he did not know how to do it, as he had never dedicated a church before, and so he wrote to the Department asking how to proceed. They asked him to work out a "form" for this service, and he was the first to propose a ritual for dedication of churches in Norway after the separation from Denmark.

He further proposed that the question during visitation as to whether the church and minister had any complaints to make, should be omitted.

In his later years, Bishop Bugge became a different man. He confessed that he had been on the very brink of an abyss. He began to hold Bible-talks in the Bakke church, perhaps the very first held in Norway by a bishop or minister. But what about Hauge? What else did he do? Yet Bugge did not dare to do this till he had asked the Department in Christiania.

Those attending the Bible classes had their New Testaments along and followed the bishop's exegesis, verse by verse, through a chapter. In a few years he had thus been able to explain the gospels of John and Luke, the Acts, and the epistles to the Romans, Philippians, Colossians, and Hebrews. This was in the Twenties. Hauge's work had already won a great victory.

Bugge was most free in his views about the liturgy. He proposed that the invocation in the chancel should be read by the minister himself, that there should be no chanting before the sermon, he would have baptisms performed at Evensong, and to make the act more solemn and impressive, he would have the baptismal font placed within the altar ring. He would have the public examination of the catechumens abolished, as not ten persons in the church could hear the questions and answers. When the question came up of a suitable book for religious instruction, Bugge expressed his doubt that there was a single person in Norway who could write such a book. How changed he became will be apparent from two facts: He became a staunch friend of the lay-preachers, declared his opposition to the persecution of Hauge in 1804, and was the only bishop in Norway who in 1836 advised the repeal of the Conventicle Act (it was not repealed till 1842); and, after having resigned as bishop, he held annually a lecture in the home of the Haugianer Vullum for the benefit of the Moravian mission. Can any better proof be given of the necessity and benefit of Hauge's work?

---

Two weeks before Christmas, 1798, Hauge arrived in Christianssand. His stay here was very short, but long enough for him to publish a second edition of the Conversion of Johan Tauler. The condition of this diocese was most deplorable. And here we shall place before the reader a bishop of a different type. Bugge was bad enough, but this bishop was the limit.

The bishop, the frightfully rationalistic Dr. Peder Hansen, a Dane, who fortunately was soon to be recalled to Denmark, but unfortunately in 1804 caused the Government to arrest Hauge, often began his sermons in this fashion: "Most Honorable Citizens of all classes!" Very biblical, indeed! One sermon of his, delivered in the Cathedral, he ended thus: "Each citizen shall become thy Hjarne (a mythical Danish poet) who shall sing thy glory as the Frode (mythical king of peace and prosperity) of our day; each Norwegian and Dane prayed Odin the All-good to bestow eternity upon their beloved Frode; in him Odin gave them a friend and a father. Receive a joyful shout even from the mouth of babes as the first-fruits of their education: Long, long, long live Christian and Frederick!"

It is the licentious and insane Christian the Seventh to whom he refers. He was, indeed, a fine king of peace and prosperity! Was this bishop insane? Not at all. He was the bishop of the diocese of Christianssand. He was especially active in establishing "reading circles," and the members wrote their names in a book that was placed on the altar, while the minutes of these societies were read from the pulpit.

Real Christianity was to him "superstition," and the most dangerous apostle of this terrible superstition was, of course, Hans Nielsen Hauge. This bishop was so signally honored by the Danish Church Department that he was made bishop of the diocese of Fyen, Denmark.

Bishop Johan Nordal Brun wrote this beautiful hymn:

"Let us pray to God in heaven,
    Who His light let shine for us,
That the evil pagan leaven
    Do not overpower us!
May we none but Jesus know
    As our Savior from all woe,
He whom God the Father gave us,
    Who alone from sin can save us?

Give us men who never falter,
    Who in faith will fight the foe,
Standing guard about Thine altar,
    So that all in grace may grow!
Then deceit shall be cast down,
    And reward our labors crown,
Truth prevail and stand victorious,
    And Thy Church be strong and glorious.

Saints, redeemed by Jesus' merit,
    Sing your praises to the Lord!
And Thou good and Holy Spirit,
    Bless to us His holy word!
Call and gather us to meet
    All the saints at Jesus' feet,
There to cast our crowns before Him,
    And forevermore adore Him!"

When we sing this hymn, let us remember that this faithful and brave bishop of Bergen had in mind just such a man as Dr. Peder Hansen, whom Dr. Bang calls a "spiritual vandal" in the Church, who desecrated every sacred thing, "an abomination in the holy place."

113

The only clerical personality who possessed evangelical qualities, a genuine Lutheran minister, who preached Christ with power and unto conviction, was the Dean, Rev. Niels I. Lassen, parish minister in West Moland, near Lillesand. Rev. Lassen was in the eyes of Bishop Peder Hansen just as hateful a person as was Hans Nielsen Hauge himself.

Beautifully does Dr. Bang say about him: "In all this indescribable spiritual decay it is a blessed relief to meet a real 'man in Christ.' The congregations slept the sleep of death, men's thoughts were on nothing but profit and sensual pleasures, with the one exception of Lister."

It is a cry from a Christian heart, this, and not merely the cold description by a professional church historian. What must Hauge have felt who saw it with his own eyes, and burned in his soul to save "at least a few"? His suffering is the answer, the suffering he was now rapidly approaching.

On his way east, Hauge converted an old man, Erik Gunnersen Boele in the Gjerpen parish. His son, Erik Eriksen Boele followed in his steps, and the Boele farm became a center from which living Christianity spread to the neighboring farms in the district, and all the lay-preachers stopped here, going east or going west, to hold meetings.

From Gjerpen, Hauge took the King's Highway to Drammen where he arrived just before Christmas. He had been absent about half a year, and during this time many places had had revivals.

This was especially the case at Eker, which became one of the "power stations" in Hauge's revival, as it also later became the very heart and center of Hauge's economic activity. That alone would deserve a book. How slow Norway has been to understand this "ignorant farmer boy and lay-preacher," whose magnificent grasp of practical matters would have made him a power in any other country, is best evidenced by this, that no Norwegian economic writer has, as far as known, made any research either into the actual workings of the "system" or attempted to tabulate scientifically the results.

In religious matters, Eker had been fortunately situated. It was here the well-known Prof. Dr. Hans Stroem was parish minister from 1778 to 1798. While deeply interested in scientific subjects, especially in those of natural science, and a quiet Nathanael-soul, he yet comes out courageously against the oncoming rationalism. "When the fundamental truths of Christianity," he says, "are gainsaid, overthrown, and ridiculed, what else can follow from this than a complete loss of respect for all religion, for all that should bind men's hearts to God? Then the essentials of Christianity, which is 'Faith and Love in Jesus Christ,' are overthrown, and on their ruins is built maturalism, deism, aye, a new paganism."

If Dr. Stroem had not spiritual power enough to create a revival, he at least kept together a few glowing embers, which, when God's hour should strike, would blaze up into a living fire.

This fine type of a thoroughly Christian and Lutheran minister is worthy of a special "monogram."

Norway has within its gallery of bishops and ministers from that time a number of strong and interesting personalities, with an astonishing variety in character and ability: Hagerup, Brun, Bugge, Stub, Keyser, Krogh, Bech, Soerensen, Heyerdahl, Wulfsberg, Rein, Frimann, Zetlitz, Groegaard, Hertzberg, Pavels, Wergeland, Roennau, Parelius, Arentz, Middelfart, Darre; but very few whose whole personality is more attractive than that of Dr. Hans Stroem. His father was a member of the "Pleiades" (Syvstjernen) in

Romsdalen. His mother was a Hagerup, sister of Bishop Hagerup of the Trondhjem diocese. His teacher, Knud Sandshavn, gave him a taste for scientific studies. He took no part in the boisterous amusements or the questionable pleasure of the youth of his day. Instead, he sought solitude, wrote essays on what he had learned, tried to paint pictures from nature, or even endeavored to copy the great works of Athenian sculptors. He loved music and played the flute. Thus he spent fourteen years of his life in a genuinely Christian home, occupied with everything that can lay a good foundation for a refined, cultured Christian character. His father's death in 1741 left a deep and lasting impression on the boy. In Bergen, where the unusually able Jacob Steensen became his teacher, he studied the Greek masters and became an accomplished Greek scholar. He read, as a matter of course, Virgil and Horace, but felt himself especially attracted to Plinius, the naturalist, and Seneca, Nero's teacher. In 1745 he passed his theological examination with distinction. Outwardly quite unprepossessing, he had the deeper and more lasting qualities of sound knowledge and nobility of character, combined with a desire to be of service to his fellowmen. A more tireless worker as minister and teacher it would be hard to fine. Young people felt a strong attraction for this quiet, unassuming, scholarly man, who seemed to know everything and to be everywhere: in the school room, in the homes, where the old people were delighted to see him. In church he preached the gospel of salvation with power borne of true conviction. The sick brightened up as they saw him coming. He was a true father to his people.

In his leisure moments he tried to become acquainted with "the inexhaustible riches in all the realms of nature" of Norway. Guided by Linne, he set to work to write a "Physical and economic description of Soendmoere." This was while he was curate in the Borgund parish. In 1764 he became the parish minister in Volden. Here he continued his scientific researches, and his learning became so extensive that he is called one of the most scientific and scholarly ministers Norway has ever had.

In 1778 he was transferred to Eker, near Drammen, where six years later he published a description of the Eker parish. His scientific interests encroached at times upon his pastoral duties, but he was all the time a minister who looked after the spiritual welfare of his parishioners. His sermons published in 1792 and 1794, and later republished in 1836, were well received on account of their evangelical depth and warmth. He especially emphasizes that "all religious persecution is abominable and hateful."

It was here, while the large majority of ministers were "dumb dogs who are unable to bark," he stepped forth as a brave, outspoken "defender of the faith."

Like Brun and Cammermeyer in Bergen, Lassen in Modal, Sverdrup in Augvaldsnes, Hertzberg in Hardanger (who like Stroem was a scientific genius), Schytte in Lofoten (in whose house Louis Philippe of France stayed a long time, and where also the first organ in Bodoe was built, and who was a renowned physician), Jens Stub (1791 parish minister in Alten-Talvig and dean in West Finnarken, 1801 transferred to Vedoe, Romsdalen, and dean of Romsdalen), like these Hans Stroem belonged to a class of ministers of whom any people and country might be proud. His evangelical sermons prepared the ground for Hauge. He concludes his autobiography with these words: "I am in my seventieth year and am anxious to leave this earth. Yet I must thank God that I am still able to read and write even the finest print without the use of glasses. I am still able to take long walks in the summer, and for bodily exercise in the winter I am sawing wood, which people wonder at, because I never had a robust constitution. My physical health is due next to God's Providence, to an orderly mode of living, a temperament not excited by violent passions, and a knowledge of medicine which makes me decline to eat things injurious to my health. I have always lived a tranquil life, without any special adversity, in a happy marriage, with a calm disposition and a good conscience. Now I have nothing to wish for but to depart hence, hoping for salvation through Jesus Christ." About a year after, God called his servant, as he sat "in the cool of the evening, when the shadows grow longer after a long summer day of useful work, thanking God, and waiting to enjoy a long, refreshing sleep." He died with a smile on his pale lips, Feb. 1, 1797, just when Hauge, who was to reap where he had sowed, was ready to begin his work.

Would that we had more ministers like Prof. Dr. Hans Stroem! May we call him "a minister after God's heart?"

---

But Stroem had an unworthy successor in Frederick Schmidt, who considered all real Christianity foolishness. He called the Christians "fanatics and fools, who do not deserve anything but hatred and contempt." And he had a fine helper in stopping all revival work in the bailiff, Jens Gram.

Hauge arrived in Eker one of the last days of 1798, and held his first meeting in the house of Christopher Hoen, who, besides being a Christian, was the richest man in the parish. The minister was notified and came, accompanied by Jens Gram. He tried at first to stop the meeting by calling attention to the Conventicle Act of 1741. Hauge said that he was well acquainted with that "Act," but he also knew of another, which perhaps the minister had overlooked, that of "obeying God more than men." This angered the minister, and he demanded obedience to the authorities. Evidently the minister did not know what kind of people he had to deal with, for the farmers present stood up as one man and told him that they wanted to hear Hauge preach. So Hauge spoke on some verses of the book of Revelation. When Hauge had finished, the minister arose, saying, that "Hauge had not only violated the law, but his talk was disconnected and his Bible passages wrongly applied." It especially offended him that Hauge, who was an uneducated man, dared to speak on a passage from the Revelation of John, which was a "closed" book which his own father, who was a very learned man, never dared to preach on. "Oh, no," Hauge said, calmly and kindly patting the minister on the shoulder, "it is not a 'closed' book, otherwise it would not have been called 'Revelation.' We use the whole Bible and speak as God leads us, whether it is one book or another."

All present could see how Hauge's personality made a profound impression on the Rev. Mr. Schmidt, so that he stood there spiritually disarmed. He was boiling with indignation and for a while he could not say a word. Finally, he told the bailiff to arrest Hauge and bring him out of the parish. Then the host, Chr. Hoen, asked permission to take Hauge in his sleigh, which was granted.

While the bailiff, Jens Gram, a big, strong man, got ready to drive off with Hauge in custody, Hoen hitched his best trotter to his sleigh, and as they started off, he gave his splendid horse the reins, so that in a moment he was far ahead of the bailiff and soon out of sight. This was as much against the will

119

of Hauge as against that of the bailiff, but no one dared touch Hoen for it.

*　*　*

During the first quarter of 1799, Hauge travelled a great deal in the neighborhood of Drammen, Romerike, Hedemarken, and Soloer.

Here the parish minister Juel told him to leave, and not agitate among the people. So Hauge left for home through the eastern part of Smaalenene. He arrived home on the 4th of April.

As friends swarmed to meet him and to hear his account of his work, and as the soft spring air lay sunbright over the fields of Tune, Hauge must have felt that the Lord had indeed been with him.

Perhaps he celebrated the 5th of April as his real birthday? It had given him ground to stand on as well as strength to stand.

Hauge had no sooner arrived home than his friends wrote for him. Those in Bergen were especially insistent. He must come. They cannot get along without him.

After a stay of three days he is again on his way to Drammen, to Eker, where Gram held him in custody for three days, and then sent him on to the magistrate Collett at Kongsberg. The latter let him go by order of the county-sheriff (amtmand). And here at Kongsberg we again meet with our friend from Vaaler in Smaalenene, who upon the death of Rev. Norman had been transferred to Kongsberg. In his account of the ministers of the diocese of Akershus in 1805, Bishop Julius Bech speaks of this man, the Rev. J. H. Berg, as "the most capable dean and minister he had known." Since Bech, who considered himself Primate of Norway, speaks in such unqualified terms about him, it is interesting to let the minister testify to his own qualifications. He has left

us a manuscript in which he gives us what he calls
"The Religion of Jesus." Those who are familiar
with Pontoppidan's Explanation, a book ridiculed and
condemned by all rationalists, will please read this
carefully. The manuscript contains a list of questions
and answers for instruction in "Christianity," Lutheran Christianity at that. Now, listen!

Question: What is the purpose of religion?

Answer: To make men wise, good, and happy.

Question: Who was Jesus Christ?

Answer: Jesus Christ was a true man, but he distinguished himself from men of his time by a higher
wisdom and exemplary uprightness.

Question: What is the character of the teachings
of Jesus?

Answer: All that Jesus taught is very reasonable
and worthy of imitation; we thereby receive knowledge of the attributes of God, His works, and especially of the nature and destiny of man; we learn truth
and virtue.

Question: Are all the teachings of Jesus fit for
Christians of all time?

Answer: No. When we read the Bible we must
distinguish between what especially concerned the
first Christians and what concerns us.

Question: For what purpose was Jesus Christ sent
of God to men?

Answer: To redeem men, i.e., to make them free:
1. From their gross ignorance regarding religion and
morality and from their harmful superstition. 2.
From their sins and vices. 3. From their sufferings
and punishments due to sins and vices.

Question: Is the punishment of hell eternal?

Answer: That was the doctrine of old, but we
Christians (rationalists) expect from a merciful God

121

grace and pardon for the unfortunate ones who repent their faults.

Question: What is in a sum the teaching of Jesus?

Answer: 1. He sought to give men a worthier conception of God, the Father of all creatures. 2. He taught that all men, regardless of nationality or manners, are equal in the eyes of God, and that they ought to love each other as brethren. 3. He taught the comfortable truth that God preserves all, provides for all, and governs all, so that we may proceed on our path through life without superstitious fear and without anxious care. 4. He taught that the only way to worship God and to become well-pleasing in His sight, is to be honest and upright in thought, speech, and deed. 5. He showed the futility of promoting the happiness of man through the ceremonial law of Moses. 6. He taught that human virtue and uprightness demands not only outward respectability and abhorrence for coarse vices, but pure thoughts and a heart cleansed from all evil purposes and desires. 7. He taught that all who would believe his words and sincerely seek to amend their ways according to the rules of his teachings, would become well-pleasing to God and happy. 8. Finally, Christ taught that human souls are immortal, and that their condition after death will depend upon how they have lived in this life.

Question: When were we initiated into Christianity?

Answer: In the solemn moment when we were baptized.

Question: Why are we baptized in the name of the Father?

Answer: We thereby declare ourselves bound to recognize God, the Creator, as our Father, whose commandments and will we as obedient and good children always are willing to follow and live up to.

Question: Why are we baptized in the name of the Son?

Answer: Thereby man becomes in duty bound to recognize in Jesus Christ his teacher and helper and never to deviate from the path of truth and uprightness that he has pointed out.

Question: What does it mean to be baptized in the name of the Holy Ghost?

Answer: That we obligate ourselves never to rely only on our own natural powers; but lean upon that assistance of God which works with its power in all things and everywhere.

Question: Into what were we initiated by baptism?

Answer: Into membership, not of a civil, but a religious-moral society, in which we obligate ourselves faithfully to live up to the precepts of the religion of Jesus in order that we thereby may become entitled to a share in the promises of Christianity.

Question: How should we consider our Confirmation Day?

Answer: As the most important day of our life next to our birthday.

Question: What is the Holy Communion?

Answer: The sacred institution by which Christians partake of bread and wine in remembrance of Jesus.

Question: To what purpose do we then go to Communion?

Answer: To a public solemn, and grateful memorial of the great services rendered by Christ to men, as well as to remember our duties and the promises of Christianity.

*  *  *

If any one should be in doubt as to what rationalism was in Norway when Hauge preached the gospel, here it is, in all its nakedness, presented by a pastor of whom Norway's leading bishop (he thought himself he was that) said that he was "the most capable dean (provst) and minister he had known."

No wonder—like Peter Olivarius Bugge, the "two-faced theologian" (bifrons theologus)—he let the children of the poorer class read Pontoppidan, while he cooked up a more suitable dish of religious doctrines for children of the better class.

He even received permission from the Government office (kancelli) to use Balle's book for religious instruction instead of Pontoppidan, to use a communion ritual of his own composition, and made arbitrary changes wherever and whenever his rationalistic whims seized him.

This was the man who used the unquotable word about Hauge, who rejoiced when he was arrested in 1804. What does this remind us of? Dr. Bang says that it reminds him of how "the children of Edom rejoiced over the children of Judah when they were destroyed." The Prophet Obadiah tells of this. But history tells of another rejoicing, to-wit, that the Pope had Te Deum sung in St. Peter's in Rome when he heard how many Huguenots were massacred in Paris and all over France on the night of St. Bartholomew. The Rev. Mr. Berg of Kongsberg could have shaken hands, with mutual congratulations, with Catherine de Medici. They were not very far apart.

*　　*　　*

From Kongsberg Hauge continued up country. Between lower and upper Numedal he is said to have experienced most unusual temptations. He was coming to a district where things looked so dark that it seemed useless to proceed. Why not take another route? Three times the temptation to turn aside came to him. It was as if the devil himself sat on the pommel of his saddle (he was riding horse-back over bad roads). One can imagine Hauge straightening himself in the stirrups and saying: "Onward I want to go, and onward I'm going," whipping up his horse and riding on to his destination. This is the stuff that generals are made of. Luther and other great servants of the Lord had plenty of that. Hauge was in splendid company. If he did not have an army behind him, he had souls afore who were waiting for him. The revival that resulted from this visit in the parish of Rollag was to Hauge proof positive that the devil was trying his best to prevent his going there. The two Roer brothers, Soeren and Peder, Peder Hansen Nordlid, and Gulbrand Olsen Vaeraas had been there before him, and Hauge's writings had been distributed.

Hauge was more than usually fervid. He held meetings on the farms of Ulfstad, Mo, Veglid, Tveten, and Vindeg, at which latter place the bailiff came and told him that he would not be permitted to stay any longer. So he went to Nore and Opdal, where for the first time he met the bailiff, Tollef Olsen Bache, who became one of his staunchest adherents, but later caused Hauge great sorrow. His brother Ole Olsen Bache also was converted. He was not as gifted as his brother, but remained a firm Christian, and carried the gospel through the whole of Norway, away up north to Finmarken.

From Opdal, Hauge went on "skis" across the mountains of Hardanger by the well-known road from Noersteboe to Maurset, and thus came to Eidsjord, the annex to Graven parish.

Hauge attended services in Kvindherred church, where the gifted Niels Hertzberg preached. After

125

the service, Hauge gathered the people about him. Some one reported to the minister that the "false prophet" had come. That is the way Hauge had been designated in advance. The minister came, listened to Hauge, and said: "Just let him speak; he does not preach anything but the Word of God."

From Hardanger, Hauge travelled on to Bergen, where he remained a few weeks. It was while there that the persecution against his co-workers in the eastern part of Norway broke loose, and between May 27-30 five were imprisoned, namely Peder Hansen Boer, Berger Jorgensen Vette, Peder Mathiesen, Peder Hansen Nordlid, and Torkel Olsen Gabestad. In the fall, Hauge's brother Mikkel and Paul Gundersen were imprisoned also, seven in all. It was rather peculiar that they were convicted for vagrancy and sentenced to the "house of correction" without being allowed any attorney for defense, in order "to expedite the business."

Meantime Hauge went north through Soendfjord, Nordfjord, and Soendmoere, thence through Surendalen in Nordmoere, where the people of the Harang farm found him sitting out in the yard resting after having walked all night. It was Sunday morning, and Hauge walked with the good folks to the church, carrying the Bible under his arm.

From Surendalen he continued on his way to Tronhjem where he arrived in the beginning of August, 1799.

He made a favorable impression on Count Molkte, who was the prefect of the diocese, a very noble personality.

His brotherly way of treating Hauge led the latter to hope that "the Count would be found among the number of the saints." Here Hauge republished two books, and published the first edition of an explanation of the Lord's Prayer as well as a hymn-book containing one hundred and eleven hymns, mostly standard Christian hymns, and containing nine hymns by himself or his co-workers.

During the fall, Hauge visited Bynesset, where Bishop J. N. Brun had been a minister, Opdal, Rennebo, Oerkedal, and Meldal. In the latter parish, a lay-preacher Niels Iversen Riis had already been at work. He was put in the "house of correction" in Trondhjem, but returned to Meldal, where the people were glad to hear him. When the bailiff wanted to arrest him again, the powerful farmer Stoerker Rigstad freed him by force, gathered some of the leading men and went to the minister, demanding that Riis be allowed to continue his preaching. Instead of answering the men, the minister sent for his curate and parish-clerk, wrote the names of the men in his parochial-book and told them that they would be held responsible for any disorders that might arise on account of this "fanaticism" that had spread in the parish.

From that time the minister, Jacob von der Lippe Parelius, lost the affection of his people, while the revival continued.

Then Hauge came, and here he met a man who both as a devoted friend of Hauge and as a distinguished member of parliament became one of Norway's leading men, Mikkel Grendahl, perhaps as fine a type of a Christian politician as Norway ever had.

Hauge's experiences in Trondhjem are the usual ones. In the beginning of November Hauge came to Leinstranden, the annex of Melhus, where he stayed at the home of Jon Jonsen Skjefstad. A revival ensued, which made the highly learned, but very old and quite deaf parish minister, Hans Eriksen Steenbuch, rise up in arms to crush this "fanaticism." He

127

thundered against it from the pulpit and threatened those who spoke at the meetings, as well as those who were present, with imprisonment.

The bailiff at Leinstranden was a real "troender," Iver Monsen by name. Long ago, even kings had found out that the inhabitants of "Troendelagen" could not be treated like children. He sent to the learned minister a so-called "promemoria," or memorandum, in which he laid before his minister as good a defense as any Christian movement has ever had.

We shall give just a few extracts from this remarkable document, which Dr. Bang considered so valuable, that he gave it a place in his "Life of Hauge." The arguments of Iver Monsen are, in fact, unanswerable. The lay-movement has never had a better defense.

The author begins by expressing his astonishment at the opposition of the Rev. Mr. Steenbuch. "Does not Christ say, where two or three are gathered in His name, there He will be among them? And since Hauge and his friends preach only from the Bible, why should they be molested for that? When the godless hear this from a minister in the pulpit, what else are they to think but that the minister supports them in their godlessness? These men have not yet been in my house, but if they desire to come, they are welcome. Then, if that is a violation of the law, you may do with me as you please. Personally I believe that these men have the Holy Spirit. In no other way can I explain that, entirely unlearned as they are, they have been so successful in saving souls. I must say with Paul: "Flesh and blood has not revealed that to them, but the Holy Spirit that has found a place in their hearts."

Now, it seems to me that it is a very dangerous thing to speak ill about that which is good. Does not

128

the Bible say: "Woe unto them that call evil good and good evil?"

And Christ says: "All that ye do, good or evil, to one of these my least, ye have done it unto me." It seems to me, my dear Steenbuch, that this is the fire which Christ said He would cast on earth. Let us see to it that it be not extinguished, but much more put oil into the lamps, that it may burn the more bright. If one soul alone is saved, is not that precious in the sight of God?

I sincerely hope that I may hear either from the pulpit or by word of mouth something that bears witness of spiritual life. "Oh, what a joy the soul would get if we began now."

A month went by. The laymen preached, and the revival grew apace. In the beginning of December, when the bishop of the diocese of Trondhjem, Schoenheyder, came to Melhus as a member of the district assembly he desired to stop the revival of Hauge, and the latter was called before the bishop and the minister and examined "as to his life and teaching." Here the farmer-boy from Tune met two of Norway's most learned men, and the only argument they found possible to use against this man of invincible courage and spiritual superiority was the same that had been used in like cases from times immemorial, where the "right" in low places confronts "might" in high places —force.

This trial began on Dec. 23d, and Hauge was at once arrested and placed in the city jail in Trondhjem till he should be sentenced. There he spent Christmas. The year 1799 was drawing to a close. A century was drawing to a close also. Hauge and a friend were in jail in Trondhjem. Six or seven of his friends were in the "house of correction" in Christiania. But the spiritual awakening was alive all over Norway.

129

Napoleon once said, perhaps just at this time, that "one cannot build walls against ideas."

No, nor can the Holy Spirit be put in jail. The new century would see the complete victory of the cause for which Hauge and his friends were being held in prison.

On Christmas eve, the free soul of Hauge composed the following Christmas song:

In God my heart is peaceful,
No harm can come to me,
For in my greatest sorrow
God will my Helper be.
My body they may chain-lock
And hold in prison-cell;
Yet shall with joy my spirit
The Christmas message tell.

The world says: Merry Christmas!
Where'er they meet and pass.
But, oh, how vain their greeting,
Who think no higher, alas,
Than holding big carousals
To celebrate His birth
Who came from God a Savior
Down to this sinful earth.

Poor souls, that know no better!
For while they shout with glee,
Their hearts are sorely grieved
Whenever they do see
The joy of God's true children
Who know what real joy is,
Who praise the Lord in heaven
And thank Him for His bliss.

The world will aye berate us
Who follow God's command;
They laugh at us and hate us
In this and every land.

130

They do not know the Father,
  How can they know his ways?
In blind and sinful living
  They disregard his grace.

But God has surely promised
  To set His children free,
Who in this world have chosen
  Christ's followers to be.
They cannot now entice us,
  Nor force by might and main
To turn our faces backward,
  Or look on sin again.

Wherefore, in Christ beloved,
  Look to the Crown of Life!
For soon will here be ended
  Our sufferings and our strife.
Let not the world deceive you.
  Remember, friends, some day
God's breath will blow their threatenings
  Like dust and chaff away.

God's grace in Christ be with you!
  With Him we'll surely stand,
And spread His Christmas message
  Throughout our fatherland.
In heart and mind united
  We always shall remain.
God grant you peace, beloved,
  Until we meet again!

At the end of January, 1800, Hauge was sentenced
to serve a month in the "house of correction" and was
placed there on February 4th. This was his sixth
imprisonment.

With irrepressible spirit Hauge, on the day before
he was set free again, composed the following:

### "Lines to the House of Correction"

A "house of correction" they call this place;
But the sin of it all is shame and disgrace.
A panther can surely not change his skin!
Then how can a sinner get rid of his sin?
The wicked, Jehovah says, have no peace,
Nor from their bad conscience can get release.
They may sleep in their sin, 'tis true, for a day,
And seem for a while both happy and gay;
But some day God's terrible voice they'll hear
And wake from their sin with trembling and fear.
If all through their lives they have spurned His grace
They will at the last go away from His face.
So take my advice, received from the Lord,
Repent and return and obey ye His Word!
For Jesus has come all sinners to save,
And truly He died and was laid in His grave
That ye might escape and be happy for aye
And stand with His saints on that glorious day.
'Tis well known to all why I was put here:
Because I loved God, and my neighbors held dear;
Because I confessed His name before men
They put me with drunkards and thieves in this pen.
What of it? 'Tis easy and but for a day.
So thanks be to God forever and aye.

Released from prison, Hauge was to be transported home to Smaalenene, handed on from bailiff to bailiff; but the very bailiff who took him from prison, permitted him to visit his friends along the route, and his journey was more like that of a triumphant conqueror than that of a prisoner.

The bailiffs soon let him have full liberty as they relied upon his word that he would return to his home.

His way took him over the Dovre mountain and down through Gudbrandsdalen, where St. Olaf had introduced Christianity some eight centuries before. In Hauge's day as in the days of St. Olaf there were "mighty men" in Gudbrandsdalen, from which "great spirits" have come, thinkers and leaders, as far back

132

as history has anything to record. It is both natural and pleasing to imagine what the sturdy and independent Hauge has thought as he crossed for the first time these majestic mountain regions, and proceeded down the great valley, meeting masses of people all the way.

Nothing is known definitely about what happened till Hauge arrived at the rural inn Stav, in Oier. Here the post-man went around and told the people that Hauge was there. As far as known, Hauge never announced meetings himself. So a meeting was held in the evening. This one meeting stirred the people so much that the parish-minister Dybdal could say four years later that half of his parish was Haugian. Among them was the well-known Ole Johansen Boeskogen, one of these deep, staunch, and studious peasant-characters of which Norway has had so many. Also Baard Thorstensen Velte, and, as Dybdal would say, "the worst of them all," because he helped to convert so many, Haagen Olsen Langaard.

From the Gudbrandsdal, Hauge followed the east shore of the lake Mjoesen, through Ringsaker, Naes, where he spoke at Bakkerud, through Vang, where Ole Vold became a spokesman for the "sect," and on to Stange. Here Hauge had been in 1799, and one result of his preaching was the conversion of Ole Simonsen Berg. This man was awakened from a life of sin and found "the truth in Christ that made him free."

He had been strongly addicted to drink, and no one who has not experienced how the terrible chains of this vice may bind a poor soul and body can understand the joy of being freed from it.

Ole S. Berg was a very gifted man, and he has described his joy in the following verses which Dr.

133

Bang found worthy of being included in his "Life of Hauge."

It is the song of a bird let out of its cage, or of a prisoner as once more he enjoys the sunshine of liberty.

> "Oh, what blessed joy and gladness,
>   Here in faith to live and die:
> Contrite hearts are freed from sadness.
>   When on Jesus they rely.
> Peace is theirs, and liberty,
>   When in Christ they are made free.
>
> Free in Christ to do my duty,
>   Free without and free within!
> Grace of God in all its beauty—
>   Free from Satan and from sin.
> Praise to God my song shall be.
>   He in Christ hath made me free.

Later in life he experienced a relapse into his former sin; but by the prayers of friends he was again restored and died a believing Christian man in 1850.

Hauge arrived in Christiania April 9th, and hastened home, just in time to witness the death of his youngest sister, Anne. Of her, Hauge wrote to his friends: "The brightest light here has now gone out." He felt her loss more bitterly than aught else he had had of sorrow or suffering.

During his stay at home this time very little is known of Hauge's activity except that he held one meeting at the Strand farm. It turned out to be a blessed meeting. Among those who came to hear Hauge was a well educated, fine young man, Jon Hansen Soerbroeden. He was a fine dancer and fiddler, and he came for the purpose of exposing Hauge to ridicule, so that he would stop going about making people "queer in the head." But when Hauge had spoken, young Soerbroeden had something else to think about.

He went home greatly disturbed, and early next morning he hastened away to Hauge, by whom he was led from darkness into light.

There is, we think, a Haugian undertone in the beautiful passage of Goldsmith's "Deserted Village":

> "Truth from his lips prevailed with double sway,
> And fools, who came to scoff, remained to pray."

Soerbroeden was a chivalrous character, brave in danger, loyal to his God and his country, diligent in confessing the truth, and as a lay-preacher wonderfully convincing. In the history of Norway he is known as a personal friend of Prince Christian August, a warm patriot, and a member of the Eidsvold Assembly where Norway's independence was declared and the Constitution adopted in 1814. Would he have been that but for his conversion?

In the spring of 1800 Hauge made a trip to Copenhagen, where he performed truly titanic labors in connection with the publication of his former works, and three new books, one of which was a book containing sermons or expositions of the epistles and gospel texts of the church year. He kept five printing offices busy, and he himself was kept at work from three o'clock in the morning till ten o'clock at night.

Hauge returned to Norway in the fall, where he found work enough to do, and among other things one is specifically Haugian, to teach his friends that a Christian should be particularly diligent in performing his daily duties, no matter what position he might hold, high or low. Hauge hated idleness. Work, profitable labor, farming, mechanics, business, was part of Hauge's religion. To convince the government that he himself was no idler and wanted no idler in his company, he finally established himself as a merchant in Bergen and started those large enterprises which made him a Norwegian "captain of industry" on a large scale.

The government arrested him and his followers on a charge of vagrancy when they travelled about preaching the Word of God and saving souls, changing drunkards into sober men, idlers into industrious workers. When he and his friends engaged in business, they were accused of being rogues and thieves, who obtained money under false pretenses.

Verily, it was hard to please a Government like that! Almost immediately upon his return, Hauge started for Hedemarken, visited Lillehammer and Faaberg, proceeded to Gausdal, where he preached at Synstevold, Opsal, England, and Kirkeboe. From there he went to Birid, where the bailiff at Svennes arrested him; but he soon continued through Snertingsdal, where he held a memorable meeting at the Brateng farm. His way took him to the Land parish and through Gran to Jevnaker.

At the close of the year 1800, Hauge is back at Eker where he took the preparatory steps to build a paper mill.

Six men, Mikkel Hauge, Torkel Olsen, Ole Foss, Nils Braaten, Simen Stormoen, and Christian Solset were the owners. Hauge simply worked out the plans, the suggestions for which he had received in Copenhagen. He assisted in collecting rags, getting the necessary labor, put money into the concern, and established besides a stamping mill, a bone-grinding mill, a flour and fanning mill, a tannery, and made a successful venture in casting church bells and—small cannon.

One should think this pretty good for an "idler," a vagabond who taught people to neglect their work!

The whole community, owners and workers, was

one family, eating at the same table. They worked hard, and sang and prayed in between.

The soul of the community was the remarkable woman, the wife of Mikkel Hauge, Inger Olsdaughter. They called her just "Mother Inger."

It sounds "socialistic," but it was not. The laborers received a fixed wage and their keep. After all expenses were paid, the net profits were divided among the owners. The peculiar thing about this particular business was that it was borne of a genuine Christian spirit, and the Eker Papermill was the very center of Christian life in Norway, where besides an almost unlimited hospitality was extended to all comers. In the beginning of 1801, Hauge travelled through Hallingdal where the movement was beginning to take a wrong course. The two parishes Nes and Aal were so Haugian, that the minister, the Rev. Mr. Leigh, in 1804 said that in Aal alone Hauge had 300 avowed adherents. Hauge had a conference with the two ministers of the Nes parish, Glatvedt and Aamodt, with the parish-clerk (klokker) also present. One of the ministers asked Hauge why God had not poured out his Spirit on the fathers as well as on him and his friends.

Hauge answered: "Who hath known the mind of the Lord? or who hath been his counsellor?"

Then the "klokker" became angry and said: "You, Hauge, have torn down all that I have been building during forty years." Hauge's answer was ready at once: "How have you built, since it could fall so quickly? You cannot have built on the Rock." They let Hauge go.

On the farm Haftorn in "Gol," where Hauge held meetings and whither folks came from far away Hemsedal, not being able to wait till he came to them, Hauge met another man, who later became prominent as a member of parliament as well as a loyal Hauge-friend, Ole Torgersen Svanoe. He walked twenty-eight miles to Haftorn to meet Hauge, of whom he had already heard wonderful things. It is a question if the people of Hallingdal are not the strongest, as they certainly are the spryest and liveliest in Norway. They are certainly the real mountaineers of Norway. And here was a real "Halling" who had the making of a great man in him. Oh, how Hauge loved such young men, strong, intelligent, warm-hearted, whole-souled, faithful unto death.

It puts one in mind of King Olaf and Arnljot Gel-line. In Hallingdal, Hauge was the guest of one of the richest farmers of the whole district; Guttorm Colbjoernsen Haftorn. The name has the ring in it like that of Einar Tamberskjaelve, or Olaf Trygvasson, something tremendously dependable.

While Hauge was in Copenhagen, this rich farmer had sent Hauge first fifty, then one hundred dollars for books to be distributed. That's "book-mission" in fact! Even one of his daughters preached the gospel in the neighborhood of her home. When some-one asked her why she, who was so rich, travelled about like that, she answered with the following verse:

> "Earthly possessions shall not hinder me,
> In Thee is my treasure,
> My joy and my pleasure;
> All else I renounce, so I but may have Thee."

From Haftorn, Hauge went to Hemsedal, and thence on "skis" across the mountain to Hol. Up till now he had travelled from 21 to 28 miles a day and held up to four meetings daily.

One Saturday evening Hauge spoke to nearly three hundred people near the church in Aal. Then came the bailiff to arrest Hauge. The people became furious. "You evidently prefer godlessness to godliness, for all godless people you leave in peace, while you arrest Hauge who counsels people to amend their ways." When Hauge saw that these warm-blooded "Hallings" were on the point of handling the bailiff roughly, he said: "Do not cause any disturbance, friends. It is my duty to go with the officer, if he has orders to arrest from the authorities; for there is no power but of God."

We now come to one of the most dramatic episodes in the life of Hauge. The bailiff took him to his home Sundre, not far from the parish-church of Aal. The next day was a Sunday, and several of Hauge's friends came to see him, but only very few got the bailiff's permission to do so. He, on the other hand, had made up his mind to entertain the people in another way.

First, he sent a fallen woman to Hauge that she might mortify him with her lewd talk. She soon emerged with tears streaming from her eyes. Hauge had spoken to her about the love of the Savior for sinners, and her heart was melted.

Then a whole flock of men and women came, and with them the bailiff and his buxom wife. They had a fiddler along who should play up for a dance in the prison-room. The bailiff's fat wife approached the prisoner and said: "Come on, Hauge! Let's have a dance."

Hauge arose calmly and said: "Certainly I'll dance, if the fiddler will play the air I ask him." Then, turning to the fiddler, he said: "Now play as I sing:

> "No more ought sin to rule us
> And scare us with its frown;
> Nor with temptation fool us,
> But daily be cast down."

This completely stunned the crowd, and the bailiff's wife let go of Hauge's hand as if she had received an electric shock. Then Hauge spoke to them in words that thrilled the listeners to nerve and bone, and when they came out from Hauge's presence, many expressed deep resentment and disgust at the way he had been treated. At midnight he was taken away and brought to Ringerike, whence he travelled on through Aadalen to Soendre Aurdal, where he visited the farms Stroemmen, Haugsrud, Piltingsrud, Garthus, and Storsveen; then on to Gagn church where he spoke while the snow covered his bare head, thence to Reinlid, Bruflat, the farms Breien and Aaslid in Hedalen, and through Nordre Aurdal. In Valders he spoke at Husum in Leirdal, from which place he went by boat to beautiful Gudvangen, now a famous place for tourists, and then to Vos.

All the ministers here were rationalists, but bishop Brun had given them to understand that he did not want these lay-preachers molested in any way, especially since the Conventicle Act specifically permitted such meetings. This "Act" could evidently be read two quite opposite ways. So Hauge remained free to work, and from Vos he proceeded by the post-road to Bergen, where he arrived about the middle of March, 1801.

was bent. He it was who with Samson Traae from

Across the mountains from Ringerike to Bergen, Hauge had as his companion the well-known Ole Roersveen, who carried Hauge's books till his back Bergen stood outside Hauge's prison on Christmas Eve and received the symbolic sign of the "Candle in the Prison Window."

This time Hauge decided "for the good of the cause" to engage in business. With his own means and loans from friends as well as two sums willed to him, one thousand dollars by Maren Boes and 350 dollars from Hans Hansen Strand, he bought four small vessels, in which he traded especially with Trondhjem and the great fish-stations in the North. The grain he brought with him he sold or distributed free, so that he saved many from starvation during those frightful years.

In the North (Nordland) he bought fish which he took back to Bergen. In Hauge's absence, Samson Traae, Petter Meier, Amund Helland, and Johan N. Loose looked after the business. In course of time Hauge's friends acquired some valuable estates both near Bergen, up North, and in various other parts of Norway. Soon rumors were set afloat that Hauge was a wealthy man, his funds being estimated at 200,000 dollars.

This was not true. But suppose it had been true? What wrong was there in that? Hauge was not a minister, but a private person, who had acquired a trader's license in Bergen. At the same time, the Rev. Claus Frimann, the "Herring-minister" was a very wealthy man, owning at his death no less than one hundred and thirty business-properties with an aggregate value of $26,000 in 1843. The value was doubled by his son, Peder Harboe Frimann, who died childless in the above year.

And what enormous profits did not Norway's richest man, Bernt Anker, make annually from his lumber business in Christiana? In the prosperous years, 1802 —1804, his annual net profit was respectively 222,000, 243,000, and 153,000 dollars, while his properties were enormous in farms, forests, lumber-mills, and iron-works. In 1804, the year in which Hauge started to serve his sentence in Christiania, the estate of Brent Anker was valued at 2,260,095 dollars. But he was not the only rich man at that time. There were many others. And what about embezzlements of the reve-nue officers all through the eighteenth century? The most famous of these is that of paymaster-general Jacob Juell whose deficit in 1783 amounted to 556,000 dollars. But these men were business-men, who squandered thousands in riotous living and were highly connected, entertained royal princes and had great influence, while Hauge was only a farmer-boy from Tune and a Christian, whose money was used exclusively in the promotion of God's Kingdom— what a difference that made—and still makes! And while these great men feasted and drank and dressed in the height of fashion, Hauge sailed his little ships up North, or walked on foot to preach the gospel to the poor.

In 1801, in the fall, Hauge walked from Bergen to Trondhjem; thence north to the fish-region Gjeslingerne in Namdalen. He returned to Bergen via Trondhjem in the latter part of June, 1802, after an absence of nine months. After having arranged his business matters he started out again a month later through Vos, Sogndal, Havslo, Lyster, where he spoke at Gaupne and Fortun. Thence he went to Leirdal, Hallingdal by Hemsedal, Gol, Aal, and Hol, thence over the mountain to Daglid, Nore and Rollag, where he spoke at the Mo farm. He reached Eker by Numedal and Kongsberg. At Eker he stayed two weeks, and then continued to Christiania—and home.

But he did not rest very long. After having visited his friends in Smaalenene, he crossed the water to the salt-works at Valloe, and from there proceeded to Skien and Holden, where he spoke at Tvet, Kloevdal, Ytterboe, Tufte, and Heisholdt.

The minister in Holden parish was a Rev. Braemer, a violent opponent of Hauge. He came to Tvet when Hauge had just spoken, demanded that he repeat his sermon, and grew so furious that he spat Hauge in the face. With his usual calmness Hauge said: "I

142

think we had better sing the symn, 'Pass out, thou unclean spirit',," and while the people were singing this hymn, the minister left the house.

From Holden, Hauge proceeded to Boe and Sillejord to Tin, all in Telemarken, thence through the Vestfjord-dal to Mjosstrand, Rauland, and by the famous Haukelid-road to Roldal, where he held meetings. From Roldal he continued to Suledal, thence to the coast in the Jelse parish. On his way to Bergen he is said to have visited at Augvaldsnes. The Rev. Sverdrup, minister at that time, tells that while he had "Communion Service," Hauge spoke to the other people in the servants' hall (baarstue) of the parsonage.

What a relief to find a minister again who was not afraid of the work of saving souls!

Hauge arrived in Bergen one of the last days of December, 1802.

---

In the beginning of 1803, Hauge left Bergen with his four small vessels, bound for the North. He sailed to Trondhjem, where he distributed seed free to the farmers. After a second visit to Gjeslingerne in Namdalen, where he bought the fishing-station for his friend, Arnt Solem, Hauge proceeded to Broenoe, where he did blessed work, thence through Alstahaug parish and Ranen to Hemmes. From Hemmes he travelled to Mo, up through the Nord-Ranen valley, and thence across the mountain to Saltdalen. This was in the early spring, so Hauge went a distance of 112 miles on "skis," the trip lasting three days, during which Hauge and his companions slept in the snow at night, and ate "bark-bread" and some meat. Soon the little stock of food was used up, and Hauge, sick, tired, and starved, was all but ready to give up, especially as the guide had lost his bearings. Fortunately,

Hauge had a small compass, by means of which they found their directions and reached the first house in Saltdalen about midnight. After two hours sleep they went to church with the people of the place, and held a meeting in the evening. Where did Hauge get this phenomenal strength?

From Saltdalen he continued up the fjord to Hundholmen, and then north to Loevoen in the Stegen parish, where he bought the estate for Christofer Brateng from Birid, who settled there as a merchant. Thus one Hauge-friend after another was distributed in Norway, one here and another there, and placed in charge of properties and business. Several others came to Loevoen, and the then minister, the Rev. Simon Kildal, says about them that they were "quiet, respectable, and exemplary people."

Next we find Hauge at Bardo, where a farmer, Iver Halvorsen Finset, became one of his warm friends. From Finset, Hauge proceeded to Maalselven, where he stopped at Fagerliddal. When people heard of his arrival, they came together expecting to meet him. But Hauge had gone to inspect a waterfall in the neighborhood to see what use could be made of it. Then they said: "Can he be a Christian who takes interest in such worldly things?" and they did not believe that it was Hauge at all. Their suspicion was confirmed when Hauge came back, told them—it was in the day-time—to get out and do their spring-work, and he himself helped along till evening came. Then he preached the Word of God to them, and he had not gotten very far when they felt the power of his spirit and knew it was he. He had taught them a very much needed lesson, to wit, that what God had given them, He also expected them to take good care of.

From Maalselven he went down to Balsfjorden, and thence to Tromsoe, but among the one hundred inhabitants of the little town not one would open his house to him nor give him lodging or otherwise show him any hospitality, this man who had come from one end of Norway to the other to bring to them in the farthest North the "living word" of God. Nothing daunted, Hauge accepted the offer of a Lap to use his little cottage which had a poor roof of peat. Now a lot of rough-scuff came and tried to break down the roof, not to let down a sick man, but to make it impossible for Hauge to hold his meeting. It is the story of Zaccheus once more. The Laps—some of them—were converted, had his sermons translated to them by an interpreter, and became so attached to him on account of his Christian kindness that they pressed forward to have the honor of being closest to him when he spoke.

Oh, Jerusalem, Jerusalem! And ever thus. "Publicans and harlots shall enter the Kingdom before you." This was the "farthest North" of Hauge's travels. He was now nearly at the "land's end." All of Norway, save the eastern part of Finmarken, lay south of him. And as he turned south to return to his own dearly beloved Smaalenene, by sea to Lofoten, to Broenoe, Gjeslingerne, Namdalen, to Trondhjem, down across Dovre, from Lesje across the mountains to Lom, through Vaage, further down Gudbrandsdalen, where at Tretten he held meetings and arranged for the purchase of a mining claim, by Christiania, and home—how he must have prayed that this beautiful country of his might know the day of its visitation.

He surely had spared no effort to open the eyes of his people to their deepest need.

He had made a noble "conquest" of Norway. Now it was time to rest? But Hauge knew no such a thing as rest. Soon he is again on his way, to Skien and Telemarken, where he visited Vraadal, Nissedal, and

Aamlid, thence over the mountains to Bygland, in Setesdalen, and to Evje, where at Fennefos he bought a piece of property and built a flour-mill as well as another paper-mill. This also became a center of Christian influence. He arrived in Christianssand in the fore-part of the year 1804. And on he went, across Jaederen on foot, examining on his way the saltness of the seawater near Ekersund. Near Ekersund he met another man who for a number of years was counted among the leading Christians of Norway, Amund Helland, who accompanied Hauge to Bergen where he became a highly respected merchant. After having visited Soendfjord once more and purchased two properties, the old manor (herregaard) Svanoen in Kin parish, the Strudshavn near Bergen, Hauge left Bergen for the last time in July, 1804, in his little ship "Forsøget" (The Trial), and in due time arrived again in Christianssand.

In August, Hauge crossed to Horsens in Jutland, to the consternation of the rationalists of Denmark. At the Grundet manor there lived a lady of the nobility, whose real nobility consisted in her love for the Saviour. She received Hauge as a brother in Christ. She gave him a letter of introduction to the Herrnhutians of Christiansfeld, whither Hauge went and stayed four days, being well received.

From Christiansfeld he went on foot to Kolding, thence across the "sound" to Fyen where he visited Faaborg and Nyborg, and thence across the next "sound" to Zealand, bound for Copenhagen. It had been his intention to lay his case before the Government Office, but as he had not in his possession the necessary documents that would be needed in order that he might prove himself innocent of any wrong, he desisted, left Copenhagen for Helsingoer and took ship for Fredrikshald, thence to Soerbroeden and Tune, to Christiania and Drammen, to Hougsund and finally Eker, where his journey ended. As soon as Jens Gram heard that Hauge was at Eker, he came immediately, arrested him, and put him in the Hougsund jail. This was Oct. 25, 1804. In the evening, the magistrate, Mr. Collet, ordered Hauge put in irons. This was the tenth time he was arrested or jailed— and the last. His work as a preacher was finished.

# Imprisonment and Trial

## Third Period, 1804-1814

In the former edition, the date of Hauge's tenth and last imprisonment was given as October 24, 1804. a date accepted by all who have written about Hauge. Later investigations, however, seem to make it quite evident that his arrest at Eker occurred on the day after i. e. October 25.

On his return from Denmark, Hauge arrived in Fredrikshald October 4, visited around among his friends for not quite two weeks, and arrived at the paper mill at Eker October 17. Then one evening, as he was conducting a meeting at the home of a friend, Lars Breche, the bailiff, Jens Gram, Hauge's inveterate enemy, reported his presence to the sheriff, Johan Collett, who immediately ordered the bailiff to arrest Hauge, and he was lodged in jail at Haugsund on October 25, from which place he was taken to Christiania (Oslo) the night of November 22-23, and was lodged in the city jail on November 23.

Being safe within these prison walls, he was freed of his chains.

The instigation of Hauge's final arrest and imprisonment came from Dr. Peder Hansen, then bishop of the Fyen diocese in Denmark. The Rev. Eiler Hagerup, curate of Vardalen parish, near Trondhjem, wrote in 1803 an article in a Danish theological magazine, complaining of the "Rural preachers in Norway" (bygdeprædikanterne). It must have sounded strange to Danish ears to hear a Norwegian minister tell them that there were swarms of people in Norway whose religious tenets advocated abstention from useful toil.

In 1804, Dean Heiberg in Rennesoe sent a complaint to Bishop Hansen that Hauge's friends were a serious hindrance to the establishment of parish-societies for the propagation of rationalism.

This was to touch the very apple of the bishop's eye.

So he immediately sent a memorial to the Government Office, giving the most lurid view of the work of Hauge and its disastrous consequences to the people of Norway, and requesting the Government to take such steps as it might find feasible to have the movement stopped.

Under date of June 30, 1804, the Government sent to all the sheriffs and bishops of Norway a request for information about this dangerous movement as well as for advice as to how it might best be counteracted.

Thus the whole civil and ecclesiastic machinery of government was put in motion to produce this twofold result. The sheriffs conferred with the magistrates, the bishops with the ministers, till every official in Norway was in a brown study over this matter. To a large majority, it was a welcome opportunity to get even with this obstreperous and inconvenient man. The Government received all the information and advice any government could reasonably expect.

These papers are all filed in the archives of the government and form unusually interesting reading. Many of the informers did not know what they were talking about. Dr. Bang says that these papers, instead of revealing Hauge's evil deeds, present evidence of the most lamentable ignorance of the ministers as to the religious life of their parishioners. They expose the ministers, not Hauge. Hauge is

called a fanatic, a deceiver, a rogue, a perfidious trait-
or, whose chief aim is to come into possession of the
property of his adherents.

He tells them, they say, that if they wish to be
saved they must part with all their worldly posses-
sions and give them to him, (Hauge) who even pre-
tends to work mircles. His most devoted followers are
hypocrites who live in luxury at the expense of their
more ignorant disciples. It is past belief that such a
ridiculous accusation as this could be made by sane
men.

Perhaps they had heard reports of the luxurious
life of the merchant-magnates of Christiania.

We have a reliable report of a great festival at Ulevold which took place June 9, 1805. The narrator is
the Danish Commander (later Admiral) Hans Christian Sneedorff. The owner of Ulevold and the host
on this occasion was the immensely wealthy John Collett. The party drove from Christiania at 3:30 P. M.,
one hundred and fifty of the "Four Hundred" of the
Capital. This is what the Danish commander relates:

"For three hours we went from one happy idea to
another. In one place there was a beautiful bath-
house where refreshments were served in oranges cut
open and hollowed out. In another place a bridge had
been constructed from a hill to the top of a tree,
where there was a "resting place." Here twenty persons were regaled with ice-cream and sweets. A ship
nearby saluted us, and we drank porter and smoked.
A little further on we came to an immense cask from
which old "hock" (Rhenish wine) from 1740 was
served; then we passed through a temple of Ceres
(the pagan goddess of agriculture), where we received
pear-juice and old mead, on to a large plain planted
about with linden-trees. Here the most beautiful of
our ladies were led by our marine-officers in an at-

tack on a large heap of bark, which seemed to disfigure this beautiful place, when, lo and behold, it turned out to be the most exquisite temple of Flora, decorated with the pictures of Linne and Wahl, and here we were served jellies and fruit. We crossed little patches of meadow planted with clover and other herbs, and took our ladies through superb groves, crossed a little river in small vessels, visited a cypress-grove containing a marble monument to his father, then up a hill to a temple, airy and graceful, built in honor of his friend Kaas. Farther on there was a park with a fine menagerie, where we saw swans, and beautiful American ducks, somewhat larger than our geese, then a hunting-lodge with fine dogs, more temples, mills, and other strange buildings. These were cotter's houses (husmandsstuer), while one was a blacksmith's shop decorated like a temple of Vulcan.

Finally, we arrived at Mr. Collett's country-house, where there was dancing to exquisite music, billiards, and all sorts of diversions for everybody. Here we were served a three-course dinner with ice-cream and sweets. Many toasts were drunk. A beautiful day. Arrived on board my ship at 2 A. M."—

Similar reports of bacchanalian festivals are found in plenty in the memoirs of that day, and that while whole districts were without bread.

We know how well-used Hans Nielsen Hauge was to such everyday entertainments, as he crossed ice-fields in the North, slept in the snow and refreshed himself with bread made from the bark of trees!

*   *   *

They further accused Hauge of "enslaving" the poor, making them "work like beasts of burden in his brickyards, paper-mills and many other establishments, sweating the very blood out of them."

Others said that "he wanted only rich people in his

society so as to get hold of their money, while they were employed by him without getting more for their labor than the mere pittance of a poor livelihood. He forbade the bachelors to marry, so as not to burden the society with the encumbrance of a family."

These well-informed ministers said further that Hauge's wealth was so enormous that if he was not stopped at once from carrying on his industrial and commercial enterprises, he would become a danger to the economic life of the country.

There were, however, among the clergy who sent in reports about Hauge a few who were better informed and who praised both Hauge and his followers as God-fearing, moral, sober, honest, and industrious people; but even Bishop Johan Nordahl Brun, who otherwise was inclined to defend Hauge, was entirely misinformed as to the facts.

To the question: What ought the Government to do to hinder this evil from spreading, many answers were given. Some of them thought it sufficient that the clergy preach against Hauge and inform the people about the danger of the movement he had started.

Others again would have them put in prison for one year or for life, with fines ranging from five to one hundred dollars. As to Hauge himself, many wanted him to pay a fine of one thousand dollars, while others again thought he ought to be placed in solitary confinement for life at Munkholmen fortress in the Trondhjemsfjord, but in all secrecy (i. e. without standing trial) in order not to cause an insurrection. Finally, there were those who wanted Hauge banished from the country.

\* \* \*

The following sketch from Bull's "H. N. Hauge" will be read with interest:

It was Christmas eve in the year of Our Lord 1805.

152

In a dark cell in the jail in Christiania, a prisoner sat with folded hands and looked wistfully into the dim light that fell through a little window looking out upon "Town Hall Street" (Raadhusgaden). He turned a pale, but exquisitely tender face towards the door, as he heard the key being inserted; then the door creaked open, and in the doorway stood the jailer, sword by his side and a lantern in his left hand.

"You must come with me," said the jailer, "the Chief of Police wants to talk with you."

The prisoner arose and followed, as he breathed a deep sigh.

They went the whole length of the corridor, when the jailer opened the door of the court room, and the prisoner faced the Chief of Police and an Assistant Judge (Assessor), both sitting at a table.

"Come nearer," said the Chief of Police in a mild voice, and slowly the prisoner moved from the darkness near the door into the daylight of Christmas eve which came in through the large window.

The assistant judge scrutinized the prisoner closely. He saw standing before him a man of about thirty-four years, well-built, broad-shouldered, not quite five and a half feet tall, with rather long, auburn hair, a pale face, but with large, tired, greyish-blue eyes, out of which a peculiar mildness of soul seemed to shine.

"So you are Hauge," said the judge in a dry voice, though some of its wonted aristocratic harshness seemed to give way before the calm look of the prisoner.

"Yes, I am he," answered the prisoner in his warm, rich voice.

After a moment of silence, the Chief of Police told Hans Nielsen Hauge—for he it was, this prisoner who on this Christmas eve was taken before these

153

two men—that Mr. Collett, the assistant judge, was to take the place of Mr. Wulfsberg, the chief of police, as a member of the Commission that should investigate the case of "Hauge vs. the Government of Denmark and Norway."

"Your case is a very intricate one," said the judge. "It will assume large proportions."

"Yes," answered Hauge calmly, "it is a big case, and it will grow ever bigger and bigger."

Mr. Collett looked sharply at Hauge.

"That is just what we fear," he said.

Hans Nielsen Hauge made a step forward.

"That the Word of God takes hold of the people, is nothing to be afraid of," he said. "If it had taken hold of the people all through Norway, I should gladly die right here."

Hauge said this in a firm, but calm voice.

The two functionaries exchanged glances.

They began to experience a peculiar sensation. It dawned upon them that they were in the presence of a spirit stronger than their own.

"I understand that you have faith in your cause," said Mr. Collett.

"Indeed I have," said Hauge.

"And you are not afraid of the result."

Hauge smiled. "No," he said, "I have too good a defender to fear anything."

The judge looked at the Chief of Police.

"What defender?" he said, as he turned to Hauge.

A wonderful light came into the prisoner's eyes.

"Your Honor certainly knows that," he said.

"No," the judge retorted sharply, "I do not know who is to defend you."

Hauge looked at the judge.

"That's too bad," Hauge said. "God is my defender

and helper, Your Honor." There was a peculiar charm in Hauge's voice as he said this.

"Oh, well," said the judge, "anyone may say that."

"No," Hauge answered, "everybody cannot say that. Would to God it were so!"

Mr. Wulfsberg looked down at the floor. The judge was silenced.

After a pause, Mr. Collett again spoke.

"I suppose you think we make rather slow progress with your case," he said.

"Yes," Hauge admitted, "time is long when you have nothing to do. But," he added sorrowfully, "it is worse for those who are waiting for me. There are so many who need a little help."

The eyes of the judge looked fiercely at Hauge.

"So you think you are the only one who can preach the Word of God in Norway?"

Hauge shook his head sadly.

"I am not as conceited as all that," he answered. "But it may be that I am one of a few that know how to speak to the common man. I, myself, am but a common man, only a common farmer. I know the condition of the people, and they understand my language."

"Perhaps," said the judge, "you would do more good if you worked as a farmer, and left the preaching of the Word of God to the ministers!"

An expression of deep sorrow clouded Hauge's face as he answered mildly: "Yes, that is the way it ought to be; but too many of the ministers preach only a dead knowledge. For that reason there are so many empty churches throughout the land, while the dance halls and other indecent places are filled with our young people."

As the judge did not answer, the chief of police

155

looked at Hauge and said: "The ministers are busy in a rightful calling. So ought you to be."

Hauge looked him full in the eyes as he said: "The apostles of Christ were neither scribes nor pharisees, but just ordinary fishermen; yet Christ called them to preach the gospel."

Mr. Collett's face reddened.

"So you consider yourself an equal of the apostles," he said sharply.

Hauge met his eye, in his peculiar gentle way, as he answered, "I should like so much to be a disciple of Christ and obey his commandment."

The two functionaries were completely silenced. Where did this man get his confidence, his calmness, his self-possession, his almost spell-binding power?

Finally the judge promised Hauge that his case would be investigated with all possible speed, for which Hauge thanked him, and as he was leaving the room to return to his cell, he said to Mr. Wulfsberg and to Mr. Collett: "May God bless you and give you a joyful Christmas."

Passing through the corridor, he noticed two men whom he knew. They were just coming up the stairs. He wanted to stop, but the jailer urged him on.

Hauge breathed a deep sigh.

"God bless them for that," he said softly to himself. Soon after, Hauge was again in his cold, barren, dismal cell, the door was locked, and a tallow candle burned on the table where stood some coarse prison-fare.

It was Christmas eve.

Shortly after, as the chief of police in company with the judge passed out of the town-hall, they met two strangers at the gate. The strangers looked questioningly at the two functionaries.

"What do you wish?" said Mr. Wulfsberg.

One of them, Ole Roersveen, whose back had become bent from carrying Hauge's books over the mountains, removed his hat, and asked softly whether it would be possible to speak to Hans Nielsen Hauge.

The chief of police looked straight at him.

"No," he said, "that wouldn't do."

The little man with a bent back stood hat in hand before the chief of police and said in a pleading voice, "Only a couple of words."

"No, no," said the chief of police. "By the way, where are you from?"

"From Bergen," said the one with the bent back.

"Do you come by sea?"

"No, sir, we have footed it across the mountains."

"And for what purpose?"

"Just to meet Hans Nielsen Hauge."

The chief of police had difficulty in controlling his voice. Something rose in his throat. He turned his eyes away for a moment. Then suddenly recovering his wonted calmness he said, "Sorry, but it is against the law."

The little man with a bent back stood awhile, then he slowly put on his hat and looked at his companion, Samson Traae, also from Bergen,—a long, hopeless look. Then they turned and left.

But Mr. Wulfsberg felt suddenly that something was wrong with his necktie, it seemed somehow too tight.

"This is touching," he said to Mr. Collett, as they walked away.

People who were out Christmas shopping met the two officials, as they proceeded up Town Hall street and swung into Church street.

"I wish you a joyful Christmas, Mr. Wulfsberg," said the judge.

157

"May I wish you the same, Your Honor," said Mr. Wulfsberg.

They parted.

Hans Nielsen Hauge sat with his head bent. He had not touched his food. The little candle burned steadily.

This night, the night of the Savior, the great festival of mercy, how terribly lonely he felt! How bitter was this confinement within prison walls while all the world sang out its joy because a Savior had been born, and all the bells sent their beautiful chimes through the snow-filled air!

Was it God's purpose to leave him here all the rest of his days?

"I am the light and the life," it answered deep down in his soul.

"Yes, yes," he whispered, "thy will be done."

Then he remembered the faces of his two friends. They had walked the long way across the mountains, from Bergen to Christiania, in the middle of winter, just to speak a few words with him. But the prison door was shut.

And all the thousands who needed him were unable to see him, while he had to sit idly in his cell, alone, in darkness—never to see the sun any more, never to look into happy faces any more! "My God, my God, why hast Thou forsaken me?" he said in his bitter grief.

He would not be permitted to fulfill his work. Nor would he ever bow his head in death and be able to say, "Lord, it is finished!"

Hans Nielsen Hauge, the strong, mild, God-fearing man, burst into tears. Presently his soul trembled in prayer. Like a child he prayed for light in the darkness, for salvation from sin and temptation, for comfort in his deep sorrow.

Then he heard the far-off chimes of Christmas bells,

first one, then another, then more and more, till the air seemed filled with music.

Hauge fell on his knees. A wonderful peace and happiness filled his soul. It was as if he heard the bells of heaven ring peace down to a sinful world.

God had answered him. He was no longer alone. "A joyful Christmas," was said in a thousand homes. "A joyful Christmas" was whispered into the lonely heart of Hauge.

He folded his hands and sang with his wonderfully rich, sweet voice:

"Jesus, I long for Thy blessed communion,
  Yearning for Thee fills my heart and my mind;
Draw me from all that would hinder our union,
  May I to Thee, my beginning, be joined!
Show me more clearly my hopeless condition,
  Show me the depth of corruption in me,
So that my nature may die in contrition,
  And that my spirit may live unto Thee!"

The prisoners in the other cells lifted their heads and listened wonderingly. The prison-watchmen stopped their going to and fro.

But outside, right under the window, stood two silent men. They listened eagerly. It was his voice. They would have recognized it among a thousand voices, the voice that had opened to them an understanding of the best which man could possess. Like little children far from home they held each other's hands till the song died away.

Meantime, comforted by prayer and singing, Hauge rose from his knees and resumed his seat on the hard wooden bench.

What was that? Two were singing outside, beneath his prison window! It was a prayer for those who suffer, a cry of anguish to God for souls in need of salvation.

The song floated upwards, like a little bird barely

able to fly. There were his two faithful friends who had come all the way from the coast to comfort him. They had not been permitted to see him, or say a few words to him—it was against the law.

But, surely, a little song wouldn't hurt! Everybody was singing. Little children with their parents and friends in happy homes all over the city were singing songs in praise of Him who had come to make men happy and good. It wouldn't disturb anyone if two simple-hearted men, who had footed it across the mountains from Bergen to Christiania, sang a little song for the comfort of Him who "for the sake of the Word of God and the testimony of Jesus Christ" sat behind the bars this blessed Christmas eve!

Hauge felt as if he were bleeding inwardly. He sat helpless, could not see them, could not send a single word of comfort or help to the thousands—far west by the beautiful fjords, far north in the fishing districts, high up among the ice-covered mountains, and in the wonderful valleys where Christmas bells were chiming—the thousands in the little cottages that were waiting for him, wondering why he did not come!

There was a pause. The song ceased. The two men, faithful Samson Traae and Ole Roersveen, stood looking up to the little window, high up there in the gray wall.

All at once a light shone in the window.

"Look," one of the men cried, as he seized the arm of his friend.

A candle with a long, blackened "thief" was lifted high and threw a warm, blood-red light out into the darkness.

"Look," cried the other, as he burst into tears.

It was Hans Nielsen Hauge, who, from his lonely

prison cell, preached the victory of light over darkness.

"God be praised," Samson Traae said. He stood there as if transfigured and with folded hands.

Now the light disappeared. The darkness of night became gloomier around. But still the two men stood there, gratefully happy for what they had heard and seen. They had received a message from Hauge, a message of unquenchable faith in God, an assurance that the light would conquer.

This message they would bring from farm to farm, from cottage to cottage, all through the land, as far as the brethren were found.

But again the light shone in the window, again it was taken down, and then a hand holding the snuffers. The candle was "trimmed," and the little flame burned clear and steady. The two men swallowed a gulp. They had understood. The great task was to cleanse the church of God on earth, so that the light might shine before men to the end that they might see the good works of Christ's disciples, and learn to praise the Father in heaven.

"Did you understand what he meant?" Samson Traae asked the other man. "Yes, yes," answered Ole Roersveen—he could with difficulty keep back his tears.

And then again a hymn came victorously from the prison cell.

While Hauge stood holding the candle, he sang the Battle Hymn of the Reformation:

> "A mighty fortress is our God,
>     A trusty shield and weapon,
> Our help is He in all our need,
>     Our stay, whate'er doth happen;
> For still our ancient foe
> Doth seek to work us woe,
> Strong mail of craft and power
> He weareth in this hour;
>     On earth is not his equal.

161

Stood we alone in our own might,
Our striving would be losing;
For us the one true Man doth fight,
The Man of God's own choosing.
Who is this Chosen One?
'Tis Jesus Christ, the Son,
The Lord of hosts, 'tis He
Who wins the victory
In every field of battle.

When the hymn was finished the light disappeared again, and it was again dark.

For a long time the two men stood there, silently pressing eath other's hands.

Then the crook-backed one said, "A joyful Christmas to you, Hans Hauge! God give you a joyful Christmas!"

Slowly the two men moved away, Samson Traae —and Ole Roersveen, who had once footed it from Bergen to Trondhjem just to meet Hauge, and who later on had carried heavy loads of Hauge's books on his back hundreds and hundreds of miles across mountains and far up into the distant valleys all over Norway.

It was by such men that Christianity became a living power in the land.

Meanwhile the chief of police, Wulfsberg, and the assistant judge, Collett, heard songs of Chrismas sung in their bright, comfortable homes, and on Christmas Day they attended divine service in the church and heard the gospel of salvation preached, while he, to whom the Word of God was everything, sat in his lonely cell, yearning for those whom he had won to God by his simple preaching.

\* \* \* \* \*

While Hauge remained in prison, the "court-commission" was to look into his case. This commission, appointed November 16, 1804, just as Hauge was on his way to Eker, let Hauge remain in prison forty-six days before it began its work. Its first sitting was held on January 8, 1805, and a second sitting eleven weeks later, on March 27, 1805. But both commissioners (there were only two, both civil officials) were so loaded down with other work, that they requested to be permitted to resign.

One of these, the district judge of Aker, Jacob Aars, resigned on April 6, 1805, and in his place the King appointed a city-councilor of Christiania, Christopher Ingstad, on May 3, 1805. Another six months passed without anything being done, and the second member of the commission, City Judge Jacob Wulfsberg, asked permission to resign, giving as his main reason that while he considered himself a fair examiner, he would rather examine any other criminal than a religious fanatic. His resignation was accepted November 30, and Peter Collett, judge of the Court of Appeal, was appointed in his place by the King December 24, 1805. It was a distinct loss to Hauge that this change was made in the personnel of the commission which was to examine him. The two first were able and reasonable men, especially City Judge Wulfsberg. Of the two latter, Ingstad and Collett, the former turned out to be a persecutor, instead of a prosecutor.

Of him, the later well-known cabinet-minister J. II. Vogt says in his memoirs of 1870: "He (Ingstad) was quite erudite in the dead languages, but had no reputation as a jurist. He was, on the contrary, known for his perverseness, his unjust legal procedures, and his neglect of official duty. When, in 1814, the interimistic government appointed him judge of the Supreme Court of Norway, the public press accused him of lacking three essential qualifications of a judge:

good judgment, hearing, and love of justice. Not being able to free himself of these accusations, he resigned in 1829, and the parliament of Norway refused to grant him a pension. One may well understand how a man like Hauge would fare at the hands of such a judge.

Hauge's case was long drawn-out.

From February, 1806, Hauge was before the Commission twenty-two times in the course of five months. Every American lawyer will read this with astonishment. After all these examinations, the Commission sent out questionnaires to the district judges of the country. Before these questionnaires were answered, the Commission could do nothing.

Fifteen months elapsed before Hauge was again three times before the Commission. He had then answered 544 questions and had been examined 28 times, and the Commission was through with Hauge.

The Government Office in Copenhagen declared the case closed with the commission's forty-first session —January 8, 1808, exactly four years after the examination was started.

The Commission's conclusions were forwarded to the Government Office together with all documents March 8, 1808.

As early as October 10, 1805, Hauge himself had asked the King for a release from prison. This request was summarily denied, based on the protest of City-councillor Ingstad.

On July 28, 1807, Hauge's brother, Mikkel Hauge, sent a request for the release of Hauge to the city-judge Wulfsberg. This request was not forwarded to the Government in Copenhagen till half a year later. The Government received the documents in the "Hauge Case" of March 8, 1808, on May 10, and May 31 respectively. A whole year went by before the

Government was able to render a verdict, and the appeal for release was never answered.

War having broken out in the meantime, an interimistic government-commission was appointed to sit in Christiania, and to this Commission Hauge's brother sent two appeals for the release of Hauge, the last dated February 6, 1809, when Hauge had been in prison four years and four months.

These were perhaps the darkest days in the history of Norway. England blockaded the whole coast of Norway during the war. Half of Norway was starving, thousands dying from lack of food, and one of the necessaries of life, salt, was almost entirely lacking. At this time it was that Hauge, Christian and patriot as he was, offered his services, and the interim-commission accepted the offer. Hauge was permitted to leave the prison February 27, 1809, and established salt-factories on the west coast of Norway, thus materially helping his country in its dire need.

A royal mandate of May 5, 1809, remanded him again back to prison to stand trial, and not till then was he given permission to have legal defense, a lawyer, Nils Lumboltz, being appointed as his counsel.

Again the Commission held its sessions, twenty-two in all, between August 23, 1809, and December 4, 1813, when a verdict was rendered. Meantime the health of Hauge was so undermined that the city physician declared to the Commission February 18, 1812, that Hauge was too ill to leave his cell. Hauge's own description of the condition existing in the prison forms a terrible arraignment of the way prisoners were treated at that time in Norway.

In the first finding of the Commission, dated January 8, 1808, Hauge had been found guilty as follows: 1. He had violated the Conventicle Act of 1741; 2. He had tried to form a sect and a communistic society;

165

3. He had encouraged especially the young people to break the Conventicle Act; 4. He had in his writings heaped contempt on the official ministry.

After a whole year, the Government authorized the same Commission to be a "court of judicature"—and sentence Hauge. The new trial lasted till 1813, when on December 4, the prosecuting attorney demanded that Hauge be found deserving of life-sentence because he had "preached the gospel, founded a sect, held up the ministry to scorn in his writings, and used religion as a mask to perpetrate the vilest deceptions." The attorney for the defense held him innocent of any wilful wrong-doing.

In passing sentence, the "Court" found Hauge guilty on charges one, three, and four, but instead of the second, the Court formulated a new charge of "having by his writings caused many ignorant people to ponder on and doubt the truths of religion," for which he was to serve two years in the penitentiary and pay all costs. There was no talk of fraud in connection with his business-transactions, nor of his having tried to found a religious sect.

When he was put in prison in 1804, he had in his possession two dollars and a half, and the Government allowed him a "quarter" a day for his keep.

During these terrible years, not only was Hauge's health entirely undermined, but the authorities added the refined torture of giving him to read the most atheistic books, like those of Voltaire.

Did no one try to interest themselves in Hauge during these years? Yes, two men ought to be mentioned, the noble-minded Judge Johan Lausen Bull, and the diocesan prefect (stiftamtmand) of Akershus, Count Moltke. At the instance of the former, Hauge was permitted to leave his jail, sometimes for days, the Judge himself furnishing the necessary bail for him. In 1807 it was even proposed that he be set at liberty so that the country "may be benefited by his unusual ability as an organizer of industry." Then war broke out in 1808, and lack of salt caused the Government to accept Hauge's offer of establishing salt-works at several places on the west coast of Norway. Hauge was let out of jail February 27, 1809, and in spite of failing health was actively engaged in making salt till—on August 23rd—he was ordered back to his cell. At the end of 1811, he was permitted to move to the Bakke farm which friends had bought for him, where he lived till 1817.

Here he discovered a "rapids" or "sault" in the Aker river, and immediately built a flour-mill, where he ground flour, a great part of which was distributed free to multitudes of poor people, some of whom stayed at the farm for weeks.

Final sentence was given on December 23rd, 1814. Hauge was found guilty of having preached the Word of God, encouraged others to do the same, and heaped scorn on the ministry, though the Court assumed that this was not due to any ill-will, nor were his writings, when rightly understood, as reprehensible as they might seem at first glance. For this offense he was to pay one thousand dollars to the charity fund of Christiania, and the total cost of the trial, which amounted to fifteen hundred dollars. Otherwise he was to be a free man.

All who have followed this remarkable trial are agreed that this sentence was imposed, not to punish Hauge, whom the Court practically declared to be innocent, but to shield the Government from censure on account of its defenseless and barbarous treatment of Hauge. The Government itself had previously admitted its own guilt, when not only the Government-commission of 1808, consisting of Prince Christian

August, Count Moltke, Rosenkrantz and Count We-del-Jarlsberg advocated Hauge's release, but Hauge had been given to understand that if he would only "disappear," he could leave his prison and would not be held for it.

All Hauge's property had been confiscated when he was imprisoned; but some years later the Government of Norway partially re-imbursed him for his losses.

Hauge had suffered as a true cross-bearer, and he will always stand as a luminary among the followers of the Lord. Perhaps no document from Hauge's day serves better the purpose of showing how completely Hauge had been vindicated than the following letter written by the then court-preacher, later bishop in Bergen and the successor of J. N. Brun, Claus Pavels, dated April 22, 1814:

"Public opinion as well as my own experience as a clergyman in Christiania have convinced me that those who are known as adherents of Hauge should be looked upon as industrious, moral, and in the best sense of the word godfearing people. From many of the most intelligent teachers of religion, who formerly bitterly resented the influence of a misunderstood religiosity upon the character and behavior of certain men, I have heard the opinion expressed, that they wished their whole congregation consisted of followers of Hans Nielsen Hauge.

\* \* \*

Instead of being punished, they deserve honor and reward. Would to God that the respect for religion and morality these people have, characterized us all. Then base egotism, party-spirit, and the whole offspring of irreligion, which now threatens to break down our citizenship and civic welfare would be much less dangerous, and the good cause would win an

168

easier, a quicker and more durable victory. This is my conviction, and I shall never be ashamed to admit it as my own."

# Hauge's Last Days

## Fourth Period, 1814-1824

Hauge had remained a bachelor till January 27, 1815, when he married Andrea Andersdaughter Nyhus from Nes, Romerike. They had a son, the later well-known Dean Andreas Hauge. His first wife died on December 19, 1815, and January 22nd, 1817, he married his second wife, Ingeborg Marie Olsdatter.

At Bakkehaug, Hauge became an object of great interest to men and women of the upper classes, many of whom visited him there and went away with the most beautiful impressions of this now highly respected man. In 1815 he was visited by two bishops, Peter Olivarius Bugge and M. B. Krogh, fifteen ministers, and the two professors of theology, Hersleb and Steenersen, besides several members of Parliament.

In 1817, he moved to a much larger farm, Bredtvedt, which for seven years became the center of Christian influence in Norway. Lay-preachers from all over Norway came here, and numerous guests could be found here at all times.

Of a man who had been arrested ten times, who had traveled over ten thousand miles, who had been incarcerated seven long years, who had suffered from spitting of blood, ague, rheumatism, colic, scurvy, dropsy, constipation, and nervous disorders, much activity could not be expected; yet Hauge went right to work cultivating his big farm, writing books and letters, giving advice, and even close to his death laying plans for an improved cultivation of bogs (myrdyrkning), building of factories, and particularly of a hardware factory, of which Norway at this time did not have any. Here should be manufactured cutlery, plane-irons, hammers, locks, drills, scythes, and similar tools and implements. His last illness and death prevented him from bringing these plans into execution.

But what interested him most of all was the spiritual revival which started afresh after his release from prison.

While Hauge was in prison, the rationalists thought that the victory was theirs. Theatricals were performed in the churches, and the celebration incident to the foundation of the University was almost a scandal.

But their joy was of short duration. Many able men started out again to carry the gospel into every part of Norway. Ministers attended their meetings, took part in them, and spoke encouraging words. Some of those who had been bitterly opposed to Hauge became themselves converted.

As the best-known lay-preachers may be mentioned Lars Kyllingen, Henrik Mathiesen, Daniel Arnesen, Anders Nielsen Haave, John Haugvaldstad, Ole Sivertsen, Jon Eriksen Bjoerge, Jens Jonsgaard, Isach Pedersen Schjelbred, Amund Knudsen Brekke, Amund Helland, Elling Eielsen, Ole Svanoe, Anders Redal, Torsten Redal, and last but not least, Mikkel Grendahl. There were many others.

From leading Hauge-families came some of the most prominent men in Norway during the nineteenth century, such as Ole Gabriel Ueland, the bishops A. Grimelund and Chr. Thorkildsen, the professors, Dr. theol. Sigurd Odland and Amund Helland, the deans Gustav Jensen, Andreas Hauge, J. S. Ulsaker, and M. J. Wefring, the Rev. Th. Odland, the famous mis-

171

sionary Lars Dahle, a grandson of Lars Kyllingen, the archæologist Dr. Ingvald Undseth, the naturalist O. J. Jensen, and many more.

Meantime, Hauge was rapidly approaching his end. He became very ill during the spring of 1824, and died March 29th. His last words were: "Follow Jesus" and "Oh, Thou eternal and merciful God."

Thus died Norway's greatest man.

# How the Conventicle Act Was Repealed

Except for a few isolated cases, which caused very little stir, the Conventicle Act of January 13, 1741, was almost entirely forgotten after the death of Hans Nielsen Hauge. Church and State paid very little attention to it, if any. Yet there were those who did not forget it. The followers of Hauge remembered it, and as these were the men who, among the laity, took a leading part in the political life of Norway, it was not long before they organized a movement for its repeal. This relic from a dark age—however well-meaning its proponents may have been, could not long remain on the statute books of Norway while the most intelligent laymen of the country were Hauge's followers. And they were that.

Even if not used, it still hung over them as an offiiacl interdiction of the Haugian lay-preachers, as a declaration that their way of doing Christian work was in reality condemned as illegal.

Almost entirely due to the awakening brought about by Hauge, the farmers of Norway soon came to know the power that was given them by the Constitution of 1814. The followers of Hauge had become a power in the land, and it was quite natural for them to use the first favorable opportunity to get this Act out of the way. The followers of Hauge were well represented in the parliamentary sessions following upon the peasant-awakening in 1830, and among their great leaders were men like Mikkel Grendahl from Trondhjem, O. P. Moe from Christianssand, and the foremost leader of the farmer-opposition, J. G. Ueland from Stavanger, who shared the Haugian view of church matters. Already in the first farmer-parliament of 1833, of whose 96 members 45 were farmers and 35 were government-officials, including ministers of the church, the remaining 16 being either business men or professional men, the democratic movement in Norway started with the forming of an opposition party, led by such men as Sorensen, Supreme Court lawyer, and Jonas Anton Hjelm, whose position as one of the most talented liberal leaders at this time is generally recognized. The first "planks" in this liberal program were "communal autonomy," corresponding as nearly as possible to county self-government or town-government in the United States, and "freedom of worship" which meant the repeal of the Conventicle Act of 1741. Not always were the same men, though liberals, at one as to both these planks, but in the main they agreed to make the free constitution of 1814 a living reality all the way through, and the followers of Hauge could almost always be depended on to support any move towards more liberty. Careful and conservative in many respects, being men of sound sense and recognizing their high responsibility as representatives of a sovereign people, they were yet imbued with the spirit of freedom and progress to an unusual degree. In theory, at least, they might have voiced their liberal view in the words of Milton, that "the only cure for the abuse of liberty is more liberty," a slogan which the people of all countries in this day of Mussolini-tyranny need to inscribe on their banners, both politically and otherwise. Any attempt to foster autocratic government, under whatever guise, is a blow at popular self-government; but it takes a highly educated democracy to understand this. It was the spiritual awakening, brought about by Hauge, which became

174

the foundation of Norwegian democratic government, just as the religious revival in England undermined the upper-class government of that country.

Interesting as it would be, it is not possible here to follow the political development of Norway through those years, when the whole bureaucratic machine of Norway was thrown on the scrap-heap. Very few countries in the world, if any, have made such a clean sweep of things political as Norway did between 1814 and 1905, and in no country has the statement been so distinctly demonstrated as in Norway that "the best Christians are the best citizens." And almost invariably these Christians were Hauge's followers, even down through three generations. All the arguments, political and ecclesiastical, which a "scared" bureaucracy could bring to bear against every attempt to realize on the promises held out by a liberal constitution were used by the official class of Norway, until after nine years of struggle the Conventicle Act of 1741 was repealed and freedom of worship made an integral part of the law of the land. It is difficult to believe that such statements from high church dignitaries as shall be given here, would have been made, if Hauge had not worked in the manner he did, and suffered for a righteous cause as he did. Verily, the blood of the martyrs is the seed of every movement that has liberty and justice inscribed on its banner. At that time, and until annual parliaments were introduced in 1869, Parliament convened every third year. The first bill for the repeal of the Converticle Act was introduced in the Parliament of 1833. It was defeated.

In 1836 no less than three bills were introduced, and all three by followers of Hauge, one by the parish clerk, Tvedt, representing the county of Nedenes (S. W. Norway), the second by Ueland, and over-chasseur Soelberg from the South Trondhjem prefecture, the third by two leading merchants, Tollef Bache of Drammen and O. P. Moe, Christianssand. It is worth noticing that, with few exceptions, all the bills for liberalizing the government of Norway emanated from men representing southwest Norway and the middle districts of Trondhjem and vicinity. The church-committee of Parliament, including three clerical members, voted unanimously to have the Converticle Act repealed. The reasons given show plainly what progress had been made in a liberal direction: the country had a free constitution. It had industrial freedom, freedom of the press, freedom of speech, freedom of assembly, hence the people ought to have the right to assemble together for religious and spiritual edification.

Besides, the committee found that those who desired freedom of religious assembly were the most godfearing, the most respectable, sober and industrious members of the church, who were the most frequent attendants at the church services and stood in the best relation to their pastors. Finally, the use of the Converticle Act had always produced evil results.

Eventually, both houses of parliament gave a majority for the bill. But the bill struck a snag when it was brought before the Department of Church. It must be remembered that the Church of Norway is a State Church, Church and State being one organism.

Before the Department would give its vote in the matter, its members wanted the bill laid before the theological faculty of the University. The jurists of the department looked upon these free religious assemblies as abnormal, and therefore objectionable. For these legal authorities the thing of prime importance was peace and order in the Church.

And besides, this bill had emanated in Parliament, from men outside the department and the clergy. It was something unheard of that laymen of the Church should exercise any influence in the management on church affairs.

The bill was laid before the theological faculty, the bishops and—the diocesan prefects (Amtmaendene). Of the latter—14 in all—7 were for, 7 against. Of the bishops, only one, P. O. Bugge (of whom we have heard), was in favor of the repeal.

The theological faculty was opposed to the repeal. So the bill was vetoed by a royal resolution of January 18, 1839.

But—as Bjornsen says in his splendid national song for Norway—"it came back."

A bailiff, Svend Olsen, who represented the South Trondhjem prefecture in the parliament of 1839, moved that the bill of 1836 be adopted as then passed.

This time, owing to the declarations received, the motion for repeal met a stronger opposition in Parliament.

The chief speakers in favor of the motion to repeal were the well-known clergymen, Lammers and Hesselberg.

The Haugians were silent and—voted. Lammers said that a theological examination was no valid guarantee of the spiritual qualifications of a candidate for the ministry.

Hesselberg said that every citizen should enjoy what was his indisputable right—freedom of worship. In the most withering sarcasm, the liberal prof., Ludvig K. Daa, showed up the obscurantism that lay concealed in the arguments against the repeal. "The ideas in the opposition must," he said, "have come from Spain, while the means perhaps were borrowed from the projects of some German jurist." One of the leading and most highly respected pastors of Norway, Sandberg in Fredriksstad, held forth—to his honor be it said, though he was no friend of conventicles—that there ought to be no restraint on religious freedom of assembly. "The Church does not need the help of the state in this matter, but must fight against all errors in religion with spiritual weapons alone."

What an advance in hardly more than thirty years on the views of Hauge's day!

And who had brought this about?

The answer is: Hans Nielsen Hauge.

But the most convincing arguments in favor of the repeal came from no less a man than the later bishop, Jens L. Arup.

"The Church," he said, "has a higher purpose than to be the servant of the state; it is too great to be the baby of the state. Loose the swaddling clothes! Let the energies be developed and put to use, and the Church will prove able to defend itself without these coarse, material weapons. It is a debasing thought that the Church of Christ, the Kingdom of Truth, cannot stand without being fenced in by fines, bridewells and jails. . . . Even if with more freedom should come strife and errors, that is certainly not the worst. There is a peace and quiet worse than fights and strife.

"The most peaceful place in the world is a cemetery. There everyone is silent. We do not lack quiet; what we lack is life in our spiritual activities." While he admits that the office of preaching is a divine institution in the Church, and that no one (he speaks for the Church of Norway) has any right to take upon himself to be a teacher of religion, or a shepherd of the flock with the same authority as those who are officially called, yet "it is the duty of every believer to edify the brethren, and the question of method, time, and place must be left to the liberty, zeal, and wisdom which each one has. It belongs to the genius of Protestantism to acknowledge freedom in this respect," and he refers to Luther's attitude to the "common priesthood of believers." "Constraint in these matters is entirely in opposition to the spirit and genius of Christianity and Protestantism. Persecutions will only lead to fanaticism and separatism."

Finally, he likens the attempts to uphold the Conventicle Act to the attitude of the Catholic Church as it found expression in the Inquisition and the auto-da-fés in their most flourishing period.

We come to the year 1842. The Church authorities found themselves driven into a "Cul de sac," a blind alley, from which there was no way out. The repeal of the Conventicle Act was adopted with large majorities in both Houses of Parliament.

It was the first great and significant victory of the democratic layman's movement in the Church of Norway. In spite of opposition from the church authorities, the Government, and the bishops, the Haugian laity had won a decisive victory, and this victory carried in its train one reform after another, leading inevitably to a complete democratization of the State Church—or to its disestablishment. Hauge, in his own day, was "Athanasius against the World."

Athanasius won—and so did Hauge.

# THE IDEAL LAY-PREACHER

It is a mild criticism of religious conditions in Norway at the end of the seventeenth century and the beginning of the eighteenth to say that the majority of the clergy had forfeited every spiritual and moral right to be ministers at all.

In contrast to these false undershepherds, was there ever a truer example of what an under-shepherd should be than Hauge? He not only preached Christ, but he lived a consistently Christian life.

He strove with all his might to be like his Master. He was a truly converted and a wholly consecreated man, and what he preached was the Gospel of Christ in all its simplicity, and with power to save souls, and this he did gladly, tirelessly, unceasingly and with true apostolic success. The thought of getting something out of it for himself was so far from his mind that he devoted all his time and all his splendid talents to provide means whereby not only he himself, but many others might be able to preach the Gospel without becoming a burden to any man or to any body of men. In this he was truly Pauline.

His humility, his submerging of himself in his work was as Christ-like as anything history knows aught about. Hauge lived a life so stainless that after ten years of constant and searching investigation by all kinds of people all over Norway, no single flaw was found in his character.

It is doubtful whether any man's life the world over was submitted to a more deadly scrutiny, or whether any man ever had such a flock of hyenas in his tracks, bent on his destruction.

There was nothing either sensational or at all exciting or visionary in Hauge's activity, only an irresistible urge, a burning zeal to do his Master's will, a holy desire to honor his Master's name, an unshakable determination to confess that Name everywhere, a sanctified yearning to win others for Christ. His conversion and call to bear witness of the faith that was in him, his method and the means he employed were all truly, genuinely apostolic.

Says Oscar Albert Johnson, today one of Norway's leading historians in his book, "The Peasants of Norway":

"This remarkable man, who with all his humility is one of the most important and four-square personalities the people of Norway ever produced, was even in childhood strongly predisposed toward Christianity, as he had learned it from the books of religion found in the pious home of his parents. He began to preach at 25 years of age, and during seven years he traveled all over Norway from Elverum to Bergen, from Lister to Troemsoe. The sale and distribution of his books were enormous, and he has told of his travels and experiences in an excellent book which even today may be read with interest. Hauge's preaching thrilled men's souls. Christianity, which till then had been mostly dry book-knowledge, with the people going placidly in the old ruts, became from Hauge's day a matter of serious personal concern as never before.

But the clergy looked upon his activity as an unwarranted and audacious infringement of their rights, and the religious school of pietism, to which Hauge was supposed to belong, was deeply repugnant to the rationalists.

The ministers fulminated from their pulpits against what they called his "fanaticism" and accused Hauge of exciting the common people to "visionary enthusiasm," and of drawing men and women away from the duties of their farms and homes. Hauge, however, who was also a man of unusual practical ability, an experienced agriculturist of the most progressive type in his day, refuted these charges by teaching his followers in the rural communities many improvements in the working of their farms, and encouraged them to independent activity in farming, commerce and industry, he himself taking the lead in these matters. This aroused the suspicion and ill-will of the city-merchants and tradesmen, who raised the cry that he was a demagogue and a hypocrite who under the mask of religion sought only to enrich himself at the expense of his ignorant and trusting followers.

Thus charges and accusations hailed down upon him till he had not a place where he could work in peace.

His enemies hounded his steps and hunted him as if he were a wild beast.

The persecution of Hauge will always remain as a dark stain on the authorities and especially on the clergy, both of Denmark and Norway.

Finally, on the strength of trumped-up charges and false and malicious accusations he suffered for seven long years an imprisonment which broke down his once splendid health.

His writings were seized and his fortune confiscated.

After ten years of investigation all over Norway a verdict against him was rendered on the strength of an old ordinance which forbade a layman to preach the Word of God in public, although no punishment was designated for the violation of the ordinance.

The only other charge was that he had used offensive language against the teachers of religion.

The accusation of sectarian activity, illegal traffic, and self-seeking under the cloak of religion fell entirely by the board. The history of Hauge's sufferings was not forgotten, and his martyrdom did more than anything else to injure the bureacracy in the eyes of the common people.

Hauge had started a movement that covered the whole of Norway and awakened among the peasants a desire to think independently on religious matters instead of letting the ministers of religion do the thinking for them. This religious revival was built on the peasant's religious training in the Catechism, Pontoppidan's Explanation, the old hymns, and all that the Church itself had taught the people since the Reformation.

It must have seemed incomprehensible to the followers of Hauge that the ministers of the Church should condemn a movement which merely sought to vitalize and bring to fruition their own teachings. Could the common man look upon this as anything but the ventings of lust for power, vanity and bureaucratic contempt for the peasantry as a class?

Haugianism thus became an important factor in the struggle of the peasantry for emancipation from the control of the bureaucracy.

Hauge's friends became the chief supporters of the peasant opposition of the nineteenth century, an opposition that did not cease till the power of the bureaucracy was broken, and the officers of State and Church (in Norway) were reduced from the position of masters to that of the servants of the people." So far the author. This from an unbiased historian writing on a secular theme shows the wide scope of the Haugian movement, the nation-wide influence of Hauge's personality.

183

It is doubtful, taking it by and large, if any man in Norway has ever combined in himself higher qualities of leadership as preacher, patriot, and practical philanthropist than did Hans Nielsen Hauge. It used to be said of Johan Sverdrup, that his greatness was European, that his own country was too small for a man of his calibre.

The same may be said of Hauge, as of several other Norwegians, like Henrik Wergeland, Bjornstjerne Bjornsen, and Henrik Ibsen, the poets, and Abel, the mathematician—men whose only fault it was that they were born in a small country. To sow the seed is not always a pleasant task (Ps. 126, 8-6), and to plow for seeding ground made stony and sterile from centuries of ignorance, superstition, and prejudice, from class-domination and top-crust stupidity, is hard work.

And in doing his work, Hauge broke the box of alabaster and poured out the precious ointment of his unselfish love in his Master's service and for his people's good to the very last drop. But, while Hauge's work was many-sided, broad as the land and wide as the needs of the people, it is as lay-preacher he will take his place as one of the foremost known to history.

Here he is without a superior, and almost without a peer. Hauge must be considered an ideal lay-preacher for the following reasons: He had a thorough knowledge of the whole way of salvation even before he received his baptism of the Spirit. His baptism of the Spirit came when in many ways he had experienced what the weakness of the flesh and the power of the world meant. He knew the enemies he was to fight against all his life. His conversion was thorough and final. He burned all bridges behind him, and made a complete surrender of himself to his Lord

184

before he started. He opened his heart and soul and mind to the Spirit's influence in a manner unusual. Besides, he made a complete surrender of his body, which became in a very real and beautiful sense a temple of the Holy Ghost. Hauge based his preaching entirely on the Bible. He drank the living water from the original fountain and in undiluted strength. He was not fed up on medicated religious tabloids, nor did he preach a boiled down, condensed and reduced Christianity.

He did not get any inspiration from other preachers or teachers. Perhaps that was why he was so sure of himself, so unshakably firm, so absolutely fearless, so uniquely original. Hauge wore no man's collar or coat. Thus he was saved from the terrible consequences of being an imitator. His recourse in weakness and in doubt was his supreme reliance in prayer.

Hauge's prayers are wonderfully brief, pointed, and childlike, and some of them have a majestic sweep that speaks of a great soul. To him prayer was a real vehicle for soul-communion with God.

His call to the office of a prophet was not printed on parchment, but imprinted on his very soul with the seal of Jesus Christ upon it. Such credentials are incontestable. Men might challenge them, but only to their own discomfiture.

Some of the highest dignitaries of the Church grudgingly acknowledged this in the end.

After ten years of scrutiny of his character and work, this peasant preacher stood erect like a white marble shaft in the sun.

Hauge began his work at home, his first converts being members of his own family.

Many Christian workers, ministers among them, are wonderful revivalists away from home, and sometimes wonderfully the very opposite at home. Some say that it is most difficult to preach to those that are nearest and dearest. Hauge evidently did not find this difficult. "Beginning at Jerusalem" was a specific admonition and command of the Savior to the Apostles, and Hauge strictly obeyed this command. The Christian Church is built on the first fruits of the three thousand won for Christ on the day of Pentecost. Haugianism was built on the conversion of Hauge's own immediate family. Perhaps it was imperative with him. How could he go and preach the Gospel to strangers knowing that his own family was unsaved? With his own family converted—everyone in his home was a true child of God—he not only returned thither after most of his journeys as to a peaceful Bethany, where he knew he was understood, but the members of his parental household were his staunchest supporters who prayed for him unceasingly.

From this home, in ever widening circles, he brought the Gospel message into every nook and corner of the land he loved. His work was gigantic. He traveled ten thousand miles, mostly on foot. He spoke from two to four times each day, and talked privately with hundreds and ultimately with thousands.

He prayed, sang, took a hand in haying and harvesting, as the case might be. Letters were written by him to friends in all parts of the country. His literary works comprise about thirty-three volumes. He started many large and important enterprises and helped many others to start in business. He established colonies all over Norway, clear up to the farthest North. He printed books, bound books, and distributed books. And all the while he was pursued and persecuted as few men have ever been in their own land.

Sheriffs, school teachers, and ministers struck him,

spat on him, or turned him out of their houses on cold winter nights. Yet he went uncomplainingly on, thanking God that he was considered worthy to suffer for the sake of the Word of God.

How he must have loved his people!

Hauge had the humility of a true saint, the sublime childlikeness of a true disciple. He seems to have had only one passion—a passion for souls, a consuming desire to win souls for Christ. He never sought any worldly honor, he never asked for any outward recognition, he never dreamed of assuming any title.

He knew of but two designations for his relation to his followers: The exclusively scriptural ones of brothers and friends. This man had the tender conscience of a child together with the mind of a master and the pure soul of a saint. A man like that is, of course, invincible. One remarkable thing about Hauge is the masterly way in which he could win the young and awaken in them a deep and lasting and intelligent interest in the Kingdom of God. It was, speaking generally, the youth of Norway that flocked to his meetings. Both on account of his personality and of his mode of speaking he was as if made for the task of calling and leading the youth of the land to Christ.

Himself a young man, beginning his work at twenty-five years of age and finishing at the prison-door at thirty-three, with a strong, well-built, erect frame of body, a clear, open face, a manly but sweet voice, and, above all, with a simple, direct way of speaking so that the common people could understand all he said, he was a born leader, an ideal preacher for the younger generation of men and women in Norway.

As there was no foreign blood in his veins, so there was no foreign matter in his spiritual make-up. He was perhaps the most hated and the best loved man

187

Norway ever had. In his inner life there was no confusion after he had attained to that spiritual balance which, like the law of gravitation, keeps things in their proper place.

Hauge possessed a wonderful poise, a magnificent self-control, with a minimum of personal reaction to the despicable littleness of the men who were outwardly his superiors but in all other respects his inferiors.

All through the landscape of his life, Hauge moves with the simplicity, the force, the magnetism, the energy and the cleaving influence of a great personality.

CPSIA information can be obtained
at www.ICGtesting.com
Printed in the USA
BVHW092140040222
627964BV00006B/151